LIGHTS IN DARKNESS

J D Crichton

Lights In Darkness

FORERUNNERS OF THE LITURGICAL MOVEMENT

A Liturgical Press Book

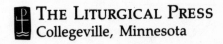

THE LITURGICAL PRESS
Collegeville, Minnesota

First published in 1996 by
THE LITURGICAL PRESS
Collegeville, Minnesota 56321
in association with The Columba Press, Dublin, Ireland

Cover by Bill Bolger
Origination by The Columba Press
Printed in Ireland by Colour Books Ltd, Dublin

ISBN 0-8146-2438-3

Library of Congress Cataloguing-in-Publication Data

Crichton, J. D. (James Dunlop), 1907 —
    Lights in darkness: forerunners of the liturgical move-
ment / J. D. Crichton
        p. cm.
    Includes bibliographical references and index.
    ISBN 0-8146-2438-3
    1. Liturgical movement – Catholic Church – History
2. Catholic Church – Liturgy – History. I. Title.
BX1970. C698   1996
264'. 009' 03 – dc20

                                            95-51104
                                                 CIP

Contents

Foreword

The liturgical reforms decreed by the Second Vatican Council (1962–1965) took many by surprise. If they had thought about the liturgy at all they thought of the post-Tridentine liturgical arrangements as carved in stone. It was very old, they thought, the Mass had been celebrated like that from the beginning, it could not be changed, and there were those who held that it ought not to be changed. Such people had been indifferent or perhaps hostile to the Liturgical Movement that was over fifty years old when the Vatican Council assembled in 1962 and already much had been happening with papal and episcopal approval all over the Catholic world. There was the restoration of the liturgy of Holy Week (1955), the *Simplification of the Rubrics* (1955), the *Corpus Rubricarum* (1960), the permission in 1958 to read the scriptures (by a lay *man*) in the vernacular during the Mass as well as the singing of vernacular chants (hymns). In addition, there were many authorised Rituals (for the administration of the sacraments) that contained greater or smaller amounts of various vernaculars. All these were signs of things to come but still many hoped that they never would.

Then from the Second Vatican Council in 1963 came the Constitution on the Liturgy (*Sacrosanctum Concilium*) which set out the theological basis of the liturgy (the whole liturgy), showed that all liturgical rites are 'actions of the Church', that is, of the assembled People of God, and that all the liturgical services of the Roman rite could be celebrated in the language of the people. This can be described as a liturgical revolution which seemed to change the Roman rite beyond recognition but which in fact brought it back to what it had been many centuries before it became distorted by accretions and indeed excrescences. There were of course some who loved the barnacles on the Bark of Peter and objected vigorously, as fewer now still do. It was understandable perhaps for there is no more traditional action

7

of the church than its worship. It forms attitudes and habits which people are reluctant to give up. Certain things have become 'sacred' with the mere passage of time and their abandonment is an affront to devotion. The cry was also heard that the 'change' had come too quickly, as it were over night (as indeed it had in some parishes) but from about 1945 there had been a great stirring in the church over almost the whole world which showed that change would have to come. Too many hungry sheep were looking up and did not feel they were being fed. If the change had not come when it did, I fear that there would have been even greater trouble in the church than there was after the council.

For the church of the Roman rite, language had and, to some extent, still has provided a problem. It is threefold. How appropriately are we to address God, the God of power and might, but also the God who has revealed himself in his Son? Is our language to be of the sort that makes him seem distant from us or close? The balance is not always easy to maintain. Are we to pray in the sacred language of the Roman collects or of the Book of Common Prayer? The verdict generally seems to have been No. Mgr R. A. Knox produced an edition of the Manual of Prayer in good pastiche sixteenth-century English, the clergy did not like it and the book w'1s withdrawn. If the Alternative Service Book had done the same I feel sure that it would have been widely rejected. The English of the Roman Missal, on the other hand, has been fiercely criticised, sometimes with reason, for its often flat and banal style. It is being revised and there is every sign that the 1996 version will be a great improvement on the first edition.

The real problem for the Roman rite, however, was whether people should worship God in their own language or not, and this was a problem for many centuries of which the story of St Cyril and St Methodius, coming from the East, is an illustration. Their move to provide a liturgy in the language of the people of Moravia met with fierce and unprincipled opposition. In the long run the opponents did not win.

Even after the post-Tridentine liturgy had become the rule of worship in the church, there were those who found the rite too rigid, making participation by the people difficult if not impossible, and one of them, Muratori, held that the use of some vernacular in the celebration of the Mass would have done something to close the gap between altar and people and would have facilitated their participation.

Dissatisfaction with the then Roman rite showed itself in the do-it-yourself efforts of the Gallican Church from 1680 onwards and in the notorious Synod of Pistoia towards the end of the eighteenth century. Even so, much that the Synod desiderated was granted by the Second Vatican Council.

In Germany, in the time of the *Aufklärung*, the Englightenment, the move for the vernacular became more pressing and the Germans 'solved' the problem by what in effect was a paraliturgical Mass. However, it was very popular and continued until Vatican II.

The recusant clergy in England, though still suffering repression in the seventeenth and eighteenth centuries, found in their own quiet way the means of helping their people to take what active part was possible at the time in the celebration of the liturgy. They have the credit for seeing that it was difficult for their congregations to take part in a Latin liturgy and they at least partly solved the problem by providing them with translations of the liturgical books, most notably of the missal. In the last decade, perhaps in tune with the continental Enlightenment or under its influence, and in the early decades of the nineteenth century, there were requests for the use of English in at least some parts of the liturgy.

In the nineteenth century, in England, France and Germany there was much scholarly research and writing on the liturgy. In England it was Anglican scholars who made the greatest contribution but all of them prepared the ground for the liturgical movement of the twentieth century. Two Anglicans who precipitated a change of practice, and eventually rite, are recorded here. Of the English Catholic community there was Edmund Bishop, perhaps the most learned liturgist of his time, Fr Herbert Thurston, SJ, and Dr Adrian Fortescue, parish priest, scholar and practical liturgist. It seemed right that the names and work of these scholars should be recalled lest they fall into oblivion.

It might be thought that music, singing, was the predestined form of celebrating the liturgy. It is *natural* to sing the praises of God, natural to sing if one loves God. As St Augustine said, 'It is the lover who sings', and there is the old adage 'The one who sings prays twice'. Yet ever since the eighth century in the West there has been tension between music and the Mass. Then began the invasion of music for the choir (experts) and the people gradually fell silent. Even now the problem has not been wholly solved. If the people now, for the most part, sing there is still the question of what they should sing and what the quality of it.

Liturgy is a living thing, reflecting the life of the culture in which it is celebrated and no doubt there will be ups and downs, but since it is a manifestation of the church and of its faith and love, we should be concerned about the 'downs' which distort the church's message to the world and may inhibit the worshippers' ability to reach out to God.

The purpose of this book is to draw attention to problems faced in the past by men who, it seems to me, were lights in darkness and to set out briefly how in our own time those problems have at least been partly solved.

There were of course other *antesignani*, leaders or harbingers of the liturgical movement, in that they revealed the authentic features of the Roman liturgy. I think of the Maurist monks, Mabillon, Martène and Ménard whose works are still quarries for the liturgical scholar. There were the German scholars of the nineteenth and twentieth centuries, among the latter Joseph A. Jungmann who, through his *Missarum Sollemnia*, his other books, his teaching and his influence, bred a whole line of liturgists both scholarly and practical. There were the Belgian monks, Abbot Capelle, Bernard Botte, François Vandenbrouke and others who not only provided a scholarly basis for the liturgical movement but were themselves active promoters of it. In France there were priest-scholars like Louis Duchesne and Pierre Batiffol and others, some of whose names are mentioned in the last chapter of this book. For England, apart from those recorded in chapters XI and XII there were Dom Bernard McElligott (about whom I wrote at length in *English Catholic Worship*) and Clifford Howell, SJ, whose 'liturgical missions' over the whole of the English-speaking world did much to prepare people for the reform of the liturgy by the Second Vatican Council. I also remember the many parish priests who for many years were doing similar work in their own parishes. But all these cannot be included in one book; so I recall them here in grateful *memoria*.

I have not attempted to give any account of the early stages of the Anglican Liturgical Movement. I would refer readers to the excellent and detailed account to be found in *The Development of the Anglican Liturgy*, 1662–1980 by R.C.D. Jasper (1989).

CHAPTER I

The First Liturgical Saint
Giuseppe Tommasi (1649–1713)

Unless I am mistaken Giuseppe Tommasi is the first and only liturgical scholar to have been canonised, as he was in 1986. We can think of Pope Leo I whose liturgical activity in the fifth century was important for the Roman rite and St Gregory the Great whose name is associated with a whole liturgical development but they were 'canonised', i.e. recognised by the church rather as great popes than as liturgical scholars. A few facts about the life and work of Tommasi may then be of interest today.

Born in 1649 he was the eldest son of the Duke of Palermo but at the age of 25 he surrendered his claim to the title to his younger brother and entered the Congregation of Clerks Regular of the Theatines, founded in the sixteenth century. After studies in Messina, Rome and Palermo he was ordained priest in 1673. Of indifferent health he decided to devote himself to study which included the Bible, patristics and liturgiology. In his *Codices Sacramentorum* he included editions of the Gelasian Sacramentary, the *Missale Gallicanum* and the *Missale Francorum*, all three *editiones principes*; and in his *Antiqui Libri Missarum Romanae Ecclesiae* he edited an *Antiphonarium* under the pseudonym of J.M. Carus, which at the time was thought to be an Antiphonary of St Gregory the Great. In fact it is a book that bears all the marks of being drawn up in the Carolingian age. In the edition of A.F. Vezzosi of 1747-54 his works were long a source for liturgical scholars.[1]

So far he might seem to have been a dryasdust scholar whose work was of no interest except to other scholars. But other projects and writings of his show that he was concerned that the people should be able to acquire an understanding of the liturgy and enabled to take part in it. He traced out the main lines of a programme for an Academy of Liturgy where ordinary people, and not just clerics, might obtain the necessary information. But he was not satisfied with that. He saw that the liturgy, as it then was, made it difficult for the people both to understand it and take part, and he wanted a *reform of the missal* and, thinking perhaps of the clergy, a reform of the breviary. He wrote: 'The reform of the missal should proceed in the same way as that of the breviary. Each part should be examined and collated. What does not correspond with ancient institutions should be cut out and what is wanting should be put back'. If this were done, he said, both piety and understanding would profit and the Mass would not be made more complicated or longer. If certain things were taken away, it would be easier to grasp the general sense of the Mass. The Constitution on the Liturgy (50, 2nd para.) seems strangely to echo what Tommasi wrote some 250 years before![2]

Nor was Tommasi content with merely reforming books. He had a theology of participation: 'Even if the principal priest offering the sacrifice of the Mass is Christ our Lord, nonetheless the Catholic Church, that is all faithful Catholics, as his mystical body, also offer this sacrifice by the ministry and hands of the priest ... but more especially, those standing around who with faith and devotion, with fear and reverence and contrite hearts assist at the Mass (also offer)'. In support of his teaching he appeals to the terms of the Ordinary of the Mass, as Pius XII did in his encyclical *Mediator Dei* of 1947. To make his teaching profitable Tommasi gives a translation of all the people's responses from the beginning of the Mass to the end and he provides translations of the Gloria in excelsis, the Sanctus, the Pater noster and the Agnus Dei. He seems to have preferred the Apostles' Creed to the Nicene. All the other prayers in his booklet are paraphrases but close to the Latin. Thus, after the elevation he suggests this: 'Lord, mindful of the blessed Passion, Resurrection and Ascension of your Son, I offer to you this pure, holy and spotless victim, his body and blood, so that to me, your servant and sinner, who hope in the greatness of your mercy, you will be pleased to grant some part and fellowship with your apostles and martyrs and all your saints. I beg you to admit me into their company, not counting my sins (*mali meriti*) but granting me pardon through the love of your Lord'. This is a remarkable summary of the second part of the Roman Canon, the only notable difference is that Tommasi uses the first person singular.

All this is to be found in his *Brief Instruction on the Way to assist fruitfully at the Holy Sacrifice of the Mass according to the spirit and intention of the Church, by those who do not understand Latin* which appeared in 1710.[3]

If it be asked whether Tommasi's pleas for liturgical reform and a better participation were made in vain, the answer must be that they were. There were no disposition among the Roman authorities either to allow any changes or to facilitate the participation of the people except by pious exhortations to meditate on the Passion of our Lord. The significance of Tommasi (and as we shall see of Muratori) is that they saw that the immobilised rite ordered for the whole Church by Pius V was defective in the sense that it and the very rigid system of rubrics made any kind of active participation by the people almost impossible, and, as these two scholars averred, well nigh unintelligible to the simple faithful. If the authorities of the Church had taken notice of the arguments of these men, they might not have been so hostile to the pastoral liturgical movement of the first half of this century.

Notes

1. For the basic facts and bibliography see *The Oxford Dictionary of the Christian Church* (1983), s.v. 'Tommasi'.

2. 'Duplication and additions of little value ... are to be omitted and certain things are to be reinstated ...'

3. The *Breve instruzione* is to be found in Tommasi's *Opuscoli inediti de beato Card. G.T.*, G. Mercati, ed., (Vatican, 1905). The passages translated are taken from E. Cattaneo. *Il Culto Cristiano in Occidente* (Roma, 1978), pp 436, nn 19, 21.

CHAPTER II

Lodovico Antonio Muratori
(1627–1750)

Scholar and Pastoral Liturgist

Muratori is best known – at least to theological students – for his discovery in the Ambrosian Library, Milan, of the Muratorian Canon, an incomplete but very valuable list of the books of the New Testament, dating from the late second century. He remained an industrious scholar throughout his life, he was a compulsive writer on many matters, and no less than six thousand letters of his are extant though unpublished. What is less known is that he was an early pioneer of what we call pastoral liturgy though his work in this respect is not noticed in most learned works of reference.

Born at Vignola in 1672, he was educated by the Jesuits at nearby Modena, then a dukedom. He chose the clerical state and after studies in philosophy and theology (rather sketchy it would seem) he specialised in law, becoming a *Doctor utriusque iuris* (a doctor in canon and civil law). He was ordained priest in 1695. Almost at once he came under the notice of Benedetto Bacchini, a noted Benedictine scholar, who introduced him to the Ambrosian Library in the same year. There Muratori learned his trade as a scholar and two years later he produced his first book, *Analecta quae ex Ambrosiana Bibliotheca* ... in which he included among other things four unpublished poems of St Paulinus of Nola. Another book followed in four volumes – Muratori was nothing if not expansive – of which the publication however extended from 1698 to 1713. In view of his later interests it is interesting to note that this complication included editions of some of the sermons of Maximus of Turin (strongly liturgical), a *Liber de Corpore et Sanguine Christi* by a tenth century writer Gezo, Abbot of Tortona, the fragments of the Antiphoner of Bangor and a study of the Ember Days and of their fasts.

Such work impressed the Duke of Modena who invited Muratori to come back and take charge of his library. He was not at all keen and later referred to his situation there as a 'golden chain' *(questa indorata catena)*. He realised that he could do much better work at the Ambrosiana, surrounded as he was by other and greater scholars than himself. In the event he felt he could not resist and by 1700 he was the Duke's librarian. He retained the post until the end of his life. A little later he was 'provided' to St Agnes at Ferrara as prior, his duties being performed by a deputy. In 1716 he was made provost of the abbey of Santa Maria della Pomposa where he lived and fulfilled his priestly duties, caring for the people, though he continued to work at the library.

In spite of indifferent health, Muratori produced an enormous number of books, spreading himself over history, literature, inscriptions and liturgy. He worked quickly and for this reason was, according to those who have consulted his works, often inaccurate, and his enthusiasm for all he undertook never flagged. His *Rerum Italicarum Scriptores* (1723–1751) which ran to twenty-five volumes and his *Novus Thesarus Veterum Inscriptionum* long remained useful reference books. In liturgy his work is represented by his *Liturgia Romana Vetus* (1748) in which he included editions of the so-called Leonine (Verona), Gelasian and Gregorian Sacramentaries as well as the *Missale Gothicum*, the *Missale Francorum*, two other Gallican missals and two *Ordines*, I and II, already published by J. Mabillon with whom and Montfaucon he was in correspondence. With whatever defects his editions of the sacramentaries were those used by scholars until the appearance of the critical editions of modern times.

If Muratori spent long hours in his library he was anything but a remote academic. He had a deep and religious feeling for the poor, the over-worked and the under-privileged. On one occasion he sold his table silver to provide a dowry to enable a young woman to enter a religious order. But not content with individual acts of charity in 1720 he founded a 'Compagnia della Carità' and backed it with a Treatise on Charity, dedicated to the (Austrian) Emperor, Charles VI, to call his attention to the urgent problems, chiefly poverty, of the time. Likewise, he founded a *Monte di Pietà* (a lending bank) to facilitate borrowing at very low interest by those in need. In spite of his always precarious health he cared for the poor, he invited them to his table and insisted on hearing their confessions whenever and at whatever time they asked him. He would never abandon them, he said. It was his closeness to the poor and an understanding of their spiritual needs that prompted him to plead for the reduction of what he called 'divozioncelle' (petty devotions) and easier access for the people to participation in the Mass.

To appreciate the world into which Muratori launched his provocative ideas it is necessary to say that poverty was endemic in Italian society of the time and conditions had been made worse by an economic depression in the first decades of the 18th century. As Muratori observed, half the population of Italy were poor and their very numbers made a concern for their physical and spiritual welfare a matter of urgency. Neglected by landowners, forced to work long hours even to scrape a living, they were much given to 'easy' devotions as some feeble compensation for their lot, and these devotions were often overlaid with what Muratori could only describe as superstition. Their religion was an uneasy amalgam of Christianity and paganism. The clergy too were not without blame. Often the sons of the poor peasants of their own village or region they naturally went along with their own kind in the promotion of popular devotions. As for the liturgy their Masses were often scrambled affairs and their preaching, if there was any, lacked solid content. Yes, there were 'missions' but Muratori was sceptical about them and thought there were too many of the wrong kind. What he was looking for was the inculcation of a solid faith on which could be based a solid piety (he uses the word *soda*, firm or solid).

In addition Italy was divided between the ultra-conservative Spaniards in the South and the 'Enlightened' depotism of the north where the influence of the Austro-Hungarian empire was dominant. As the century drew on emperors showed an ever-increasing tendency to interfere with the intimate affairs of church life, a tendency which reached its climax in the work of the Sacristan-Emperor, Joseph II. He and others ruthlessly cut away devotions, chapels and popular celebrations of the people, to their great discontent, and thus did in an authoritarian manner what Muratori hoped would be done before this by the Church authorities themselves. Where he differed, and radically, was that he wanted to educate and persuade so that the people, seeing where the centre of Christian faith and practice lay, would assist at Mass with understanding and shed the superstitious elements of their devotions. In fact the situation showed some signs of improvement just before the rationalism of the French Revolution swept into Italy and Napoleon tried to continue the policies of the Austro-Hungarian emperors, now divested of power.

Muratori first expounded his views on liturgy and devotions in his *Della Regolata Devozione dei Cristiani*[1] which appeared in 1747 in Venice, the usual place of publication for 'way out' books. He anticipated opposition and tried to fend it off by consulting his friend Cardinal Fortunato Tamburini, who worked in the Curia and was an intimate of Benedict XIV. Muratori indeed hoped that the pope would give the book his approbation but Benedict knew his world. He saw that Muratori was 'surrounded by dogs who only hold back out of respect for me, knowing the high esteem I have for him'. Tamburini however not only read the book but suggested a number of changes, all of which Muratori incorporated. Even so the book caused something of a furore.

He begins by describing what he regarded as the religious decadence of his time. Religion is 'noble and holy' but even so it suffers from defects and excesses, though these are of course to be attributed to human failures. As to defects, the only one he lights upon is a suspicion that there were some opposed to religion itself. The rationalism of the Enlightenment had been percolating into Italy for some time, especially among the upper classes. The first excess he mentions was the superstition mixed up with the popular devotions which led the people to arbitrary and superficial aspects of religion and worship.

As for the pompous, over-elaborate and long drawn out liturgical functions he thought the time and energy spent on them was 'prejudicial to the temporal welfare of the state'. Here was a touch of the Enlightenment mentality. Processions and popular missions could be conducive to devotion but in excess (and Muratori thought there was too much of both) 'they take away the people from their work, which is necessary for their livelihood'. This was something that touched Muratori's heart and that is why, as we shall see later, he was strongly in favour of the reduction in number of 'days of obligation'.

It will be seen that in a country like Italy that was so traditionalist in its religious attitudes and where the higher clergy, including bishops, had little contact with the poor, Muratori's charges were not likely to earn him any popularity. Nor did they. There were indeed many dogs surrounding him, only too ready to find good reason, as they thought, to attack him.

A summary of the book, by Enrico Cattaneo[2], reveals Muratori's main points as well as his fundamental sanity.

1. The devotion God wants of us if we are to be true Christians. In this context Muratori deals with superstitions. (Chapter I).

2. Devotion to God, Father, Son and Holy Spirit. This of course was the centre of everything and Muratori thought this certain devotions, concerned with St Mary and other saints, with their 'superstitious' elements, obscured this central truth. (cc II-IV).

3. Devotion must be accompanied by good works, founded on the theological virtues faith, hope and charity (V-IX).

4. Prayer and the virtues that should accompany it, viz. self-denial, humility, patience, Penance (sacrament and virtue) and its fruits in good living (X-XIV).

5. The Mass and the way people should participate in it (XIV-XIX).

6. Devotions to Mary and the saints (XX-XXV).

Although Muratori is emphatic that he is not producing yet another book on the spiritual life of which he says there are plenty written by saints and other holy people, what he gives in his book is a treatise on the Christian life as it should be lived by ordinary people. No doubt he hoped that the clergy would use it to convey its message to the poor he loved and who were largely illiterate. But he was also concerned about 'the superabundance of devotions', and to make his point he retails a story he must have got from some French source.

Once there was a prudent and worthy gentleman who was at Cambrai visiting Fénelon. He is allowed to sit in on an instruction given by the archbishop to two noble Calvinist (?) ladies from England. He speaks to them of the prayers of the Church and when he had finished he asked them what they thought of what he had said. 'Monseigneur' one replied, 'The religion of Calvin seems to me too naked; the Roman Catholic religion seems over-dressed'. And she went on (though one wonders whether

Muratori has not adorned the tale) that she had noticed a great abundance and variety of religious orders, rites and devotions and there are too many vestments and ornaments. Fénelon hardly answers the question: all these things have nothing unworthy (*indecenza*) about them or anything opposed to the doctrines of the Church. In any case, devotions are free and not imposed on anyone.

This leads Muratori to expatiate on devotions once again. In secular life people are always seeking novelties and the same happens in the world of piety. They are sometimes sincere but sometimes they practice them in emulation of others or for other (unworthy) reasons. One trouble however is that the Church has inherited a whole baggage of devotions and there are, at all times, people who have invented (*inventate*) new ones and continue to do so. We must not be surprised then that 'the old and the new combine to make a system that seems rather to oppress than to adorn our holy religion' (p 435). Then he returns to his 'ordinary people' who must be occupied with the pursuits that are proper to their condition and, as he says elsewhere, desperately trying to scratch a living. To conclude, he returns to what is his main concern: 'nothing can compare with the Mass attended in the proper way and completed with communion … it includes the best of the prayers (of the Church) and God has made participation in it easy and within the capacity of all, whether poor or rich, (p 435).

Easy participation? It seemed unobtainable at the time. Yet that is what Muratori really wanted with some use of the vernacular in the celebration of the Mass, at least for the scripture readings. This was one of the suggestions that Tamburini had eliminated from the first draft of the *Della Regolata Devozione*; he knew that the pope would not and could not accept that. The question of the liturgy or even part of the liturgy being in the language of the people aroused the fiercest opposition. The words of the Mass, all the words, (in Latin) were sacred and must not be exposed to the vulgar herd. What then of these laypeople, at least in the middle and upper classes, who *did* know Latin? Muratori ventured to say that what was all right for them was all right for the 'ignorant'. Might they not hear some of the sacred words even if they were in Italian?

He illustrated his views (and his very modest suggestion) by recording an experience in the Austrian Tyrol. He was travelling there and one Sunday went to the parish church to hear 'or' to celebrate Mass (that 'or' is interesting). He arrived as the parish priest was beginning to say Mass which proceeded in the usual way until the gospel. This, as was the custom of the time, he read in Latin at the left hand corner of the altar. Having done so, he left the altar, came down to the altar rail and 'in a loud voice read from a book in German the same gospel for that is the native language of the people' (pp 441, 442). The same custom, he said, was to be found in Dalmatia (now Yugoslavia; if it still exists when this is published) and Moravia (now the Czech republic).

When Tamburini read this he exploded. If that much was grant-ed the people would murmur against the Church (though he failed to observe that this had not happened in Austria, Dalmatia and Moravia) and they would go on to say that if such consolation was to be found in the Mass, they would demand that the whole of it should be in their own language and that was out of the question. Muratori gave way and contented him-self with saying that the 'ignorant faithful', who he could not stop himself from saying were 'the greatest part of the people', should come to an understanding of 'the holy words of the gospel and the heavenly teaching they contain' by some other way. One was that the parish clergy should explain the gospel on Sundays and then, recalling what the pope Benedict XIV had ordered, that preachers must only quote the Bible in Latin, Muratori with some sarcasm asked: 'What then? Is it only the learned who are to profit from the gospel message and are the rest of the people to be condemned never to understand the words of life? (p 443).

So he sought the 'other way' and translated the Ordinary of the Mass. Commentating on his own efforts he wrote: 'Since it is a great difficulty to conceive and maintain devotion in their hearts (during Mass) and if ignorance of Latin prevents them from un-derstanding the beauty of the holy prayers that the Church for just reasons continues to recite in that language, here it is my de-sire to expound the Mass and its sacred and wonderful words for those who do not know Latin and do not understand what the priest, *in the name of all*, asks of God in the celebration of the Mass.[3] Then he repeats in the context of the Mass what he had said about the use of Latin quotations in sermons: if there are those who understand Latin and can read and appreciate the meaning of the words it seems only right that those of lesser attainments (*ingegni*) should be able to do likewise. The result will be an increase of their devotion, and this will in no way lessen the nobility of this great celebration (ibid).

In another place he shows that he has a sound grasp of the central mystery of the Mass. At a time, and not only in Italy, when the devotional way of hearing Mass was to meditate on the Passion of Christ (urged by papal and other documents for another two centuries to come), Muratori, perhaps as a result of his pondering on the texts of the ancient sacramentaries, suggested to the people that they should give 'a devout attention to the "divine mysteries" re-presented in the Mass as they were at the Last Supper, namely the passion, resurrection and ascension of the Lord as well as to the real presence of the Redeemer'. This emphasis on the resurrection and the ascension, for all that they are mentioned in the Roman Canon, was unusual for the time though there were persecuted priests in England who made the same emphasis.[4]

On the broader lines he wished the people to understand what are the great actions of the Mass, the offertory, the consecration and the communion and to participate at these times as well as they could. Understandably, he put most of the emphasis on holy communion and thus became involved in another controversy. At the time and for long afterwards people regularly received communion before Mass or after it and altogether apart from it. Muratori saw and said that this was an anomaly. Benedict XIV was with him in this and issued an encyclical on the matter though, as in so many papal pronouncements, there was a great deal of 'on the one hand' and 'on the other', (text, p 447, n 29). He did however insist that communion should be given from the bread consecrated at the Mass the people attended – a ruling that, alas, is not always observed to this day. Popes may decree and the parish clergy do what they like.

For his part while wholly agreeing with the papal instruction, Muratori always kept in mind the poor, the workers of various sorts, those who had to return to their farms or places of work, sometimes even in Italy, at great distances away from the church. In those circumstances other arrangements might be made so as not to delay them. Great numbers going to communion, as at Easter, would prolong the celebration and then communion might be given to some apart from but in close connection with the Mass (pp 447, n 30).

As has been said above, certain religious practices, tolerable in themselves, like processions and popular missions when used to excess were detrimental to the welfare of the poor people for 'they take them away from their work which is necessary for their livelihood'. This was something that touched Muratori deeply and led him into another and bitter controversy. It was about the number of feasts of obligation, about sixty in the year to which were to be added the fifty-two Sundays, which not only required attendance at Mass but the cessation of the work termed 'servile' in which the vast majority of the people were engaged. This rule cost them loss of production which in the many lean years of the century could be serious, and, if they were able to sell their produce, loss of income.

A terrific row broke out which involved bishops, cardinals, the pope and Muratori! His views on the reduction of the number of obligatory feasts, which were shared by others, were fiercely rejected especially by Cardinal Querini, Bishop of Brescia and the Archbishop of Milan, among others. The matter was put before the pope who although he had sympathy with the Muratorian view, realised that if he decided in his favour, he, the pope, would become the target of criticism. He decided to temporise; bishops in their own diocese were to decide what feast days should be suppressed and what celebrated. In other words, everyone stood to his own position. Only for a time. When the Josephite regulations were imposed on the Austrian territories in northern Italy, the number of feasts of obligation was reduced whatever bishops or pope wanted.

Muratori was also of the opinion that the numbers of priests, churches and houses of religious should be reduced. In towns and cities where there was already a sufficiency of churches and religious houses no more should be built. He would have applied the rule to whole dioceses. There were too many priests and too many religious, often doing very little. But he was only Muratori and things went on as before.

Six years after the *Della Regolata Devozione dei Cristiani*, Muratori died. The book had been published under a pseudonym which was soon pierced and he became the target of many attacks from bishops and even cardinals. The mood of the time was very conservative; what had been done time out of mind (certain devotional habits) must be right because they were familiar and old. The church in Italy was unexpectedly obsessed by Jansenism (though hardly of the theological sort) which infiltrated from France, and, very surprisingly, by the fear of Protestantism which had difficulty in putting down roots there. Church authorities were more realistic when confronted with the Enlightenment which was far more dangerous than Jansenism or Protestantism. However, the Church in Italy felt itself under attack from foreign elements and its leaders decided that no change in anything must be that policy. Only this could fend off the enemy. Muratori's modest pleas for some liturgical change were therefore regarded by some with horror.

It seems however that he made a tactical error in attacking devotions which formed so large a part of the religious life of the unlettered at the time. Praying in front of and perhaps close to a statue of the Blessed Virgin Mary holding the infant Jesus (as was the almost invariable custom), the people could feel that they were in contact with a religious reality which no doubt they vaguely realised was present in a different way in the Mass but which was remote from them. And prayers to various saints and pilgrimages to their shrines for healing was about the only kind of 'medicine' available to them. When Joseph II tried to stop processions and pilgrimages and destroy shrines, the people protested loudly, and when the Napoleonic wars were over everything returned to its former state. Muratori was also unwise to criticise the pomp and ceremony of certain liturgical celebrations. These were mostly episcopal so bishops and chapters of canons felt they were directly under attack. Nevertheless, the times were not propitious for liturgical change and it is possible that even if Muratori had not attacked excessive ceremonial and quasi-superstitious devotions, his views would have been rejected. It is ironical that all the arguments against a vernacular liturgy (the stability of Latin as a reflection of the stability of the faith, Latin as a sacred language, the confusion caused to tourists(!) and the difficulties of translation ...) were rehearsed by popes and bishops year after year *usque ad nauseam*. It is to be hoped that the dreadful news of the Second Vatican Council has been withheld from them in their celestial bliss.

It may seem that Muratori's efforts had little influence in his time though his *Della Regolata Devozione* was translated into other European languages and a recent historian sees his book as a 'symbol of the Catholic reforming ideals of the later eighteenth century'.[5] Moreover he can be seen as being in a certain tradition, reaching back to the wholly orthodox Tommasi (now canonised) and on to Rosmini in the century after him. All of them may seem to have been prophets crying in the wilderness but they testify to the unsatisfactory nature of the post-Tridentine reform which made any sort of change so difficult, something we have experienced in our own time. Both Tommasi and Rosmini had a deep concern for the lowly of this world and this was strikingly true of Muratori. Of him Owen Chadwick has movingly written: 'Muratori was the finest type of Catholic reformer in the eighteenth century; where critical intelligence assailed popular superstition at the same time as a pastoral heart longed for the well-being of a people's religion'.[6]

Bibliography

See Enrico Cattaneo, *Il Culto Cristiano in Occidents* (C.L.V. Edizioni Liturgiche, Rome, 1978) who gives copious extracts from Muratori's pastoral-liturgical writings. Cf pp 431ff. See also O. Chadwick's book already referred to, pp 395-402).

Notes

1. Which may be translated: *A Christian's Well-ordered Devotion*.

2. *Il Culto Cristiano in Occidente*, (1978), p 434.

3. Italics mine. Muratori also taught the people that they offer with the priest who represents Christ and them.

4. See my *Worship in a Hidden Church* (Dublin, 1988), pp 27-28.

5. Owen Chadwick, *The Popes and the European Revolution* (OUP, 1981), p 400.

6. ibid, p 397.

Antonio Rosmini (1797-1855)
A nineteenth-century
Pastoral Liturgist

In 1832 Rosmini wrote a book called *Delle Cinque Piaghe della Chiesa* (The Five Wounds of the Church) which however did not appear until 1846, in the false dawn of the 'liberalism' of Pius IX's first years. It was put on the Index of Prohibited Books fairly promptly in 1849, was removed a year before his death and with his many other works was put back again in 1887/8.[1] They were taken off again in more recent years just before the total abolition of the Index which had become completely discredited and useless. Contrary to what was intended, Rosmini as a thinker and a writer gained a certain notoriety which in the long run has done him no harm. A philosopher, he had an independent and very searching mind and he had read very widely. With the encouragement of Pius VIII he undertook a translation of the *Summa Theologiae* of St Thomas though later he ranged far away from him. No doubt his principal philosophical works will reveal his quality when they are published in English.

Thinker though he was, Rosmini was deeply concerned about the condition of the Church in his time. Italy and Rome itself had been ravaged by Napoleon. Not only did he transport great quantities of Italian art to France but he caused disarray (called 'liberation'!) in every department of life. Among the casualties were the theological schools which for some years were closed and no serious study was possible. Two 'wounds' of the Church were, first, the lack of education among the clergy and the state 'nomination' of bishops which in effect meant Spain and Austria-Hungary and so of course in the Austrian possessions of northern Italy and those of Spain in the south. It would take another revolution, the unification of Italy in 1870 and changes in Europe and elsewhere, to bring this harmful system to an end.

The third 'wound', in fact the first chapter of the book, was the

25

division or separation of the laity from the clergy in worship. Rosmini sought to remedy this, hence his chapter on the liturgy.

He goes far back to principles, to the nature of the human being. He is a unity, a body-soul creature and the salvation process set out in the Bible is concerned with the 'whole person'. The Gospel is both word and action and is addressed to the whole person. Christ said, 'go and teach ...' but he also told his disciples to baptise and at the Last Supper he said, 'Do this...'. This is the message which meets the needs of human beings who are thus able to respond to it by word and action. Rosmini sees worship as a consequence of the incarnation when the Word of God became human so that we might respond to him in a human way. For Rosmini insists that worship is a human action, in the full sense, even if its content is divine with a re-creative power 'for the renewal of the earth and the revitalisation of the human race'. The liturgy, of course including all the sacraments, consists, yes, of words that reveal God's hidden action – as some later liturgists would say, it is an epiphany of the saving mystery of Christ – but it is also the means by which we are able to live the message in a manner that is harmonious with human nature. Rosmini's insights here are quite remarkable, especially when we take into account the poverty of the theology of the time. Although he is using the terms and vocabulary of his era, he has penetrated to the deeper meaning of the liturgy which would not be seen for nearly a hundred years.

Rosmini's views on the liturgy were based on an ecclesiology that was rare at the time. For him the Church is the mystical body of Christ and, as if that doctrine might seem remote, he made it more concrete by adding that it is a 'family in the supernatural order' brought into existence by baptism, a family in which 'the Creator becomes the Father of all (the baptised) so that 'the Church is nothing other than the family of God'. Furthermore (and anticipating the Second Vatican Council!) he sees the whole Church as a sacramental reality, structured by the sacraments and coming into action through their celebration. This has consequences for the people who in baptism receive a share in the priesthood of Christ and have a right to receive, e.g. the sacraments, and to exercise their right in celebration: 'Rosmini uncovered the great (and traditional) truth of the common priesthood of the faithful'.[2] This indeed a truth that has been forgotten for some long time and I do not think Rosmini had read his St Thomas in vain.[3]

One consequence of this is that the baptised laity have a part to play in the celebration of the liturgy. In words that seem to be echoed in Pius XI's *Divini cultus* (1928) and in the Constitution of the Liturgy (no 48) Rosmini said that the liturgy is 'not a spectacle for the people to behold' ('not to be silent spectators'; Constitution on Liturgy, no 48); they are intended 'not to be present simply to look at what is happening'. Rather they are meant to be 'genuinely participating in this drama of religious worship'. Still speaking of what was intended (but, the implication is that it was no longer happening), he says that the people were themselves to be an important element in worship, sometimes receiving as they do primarily in the sacraments but at other times united with the priest they act with the clergy, 'as in prayers they said, in their responses to the priests, in the exchange of peace, at the offertory, and even as ministers of the sacrament at weddings'. Sometimes the clergy act as Christ's representative, at others they mix with the laity, they pray with them awaiting (God's) 'mysterious divine action'. Thus he concludes, 'The sublime worship of holy church is a single action, the result of orderly, reasonable accord working to bring about a single, combined homage' (pp 10–11). Rosmini backs this up with a reference to Matthew 18:20, 'Where two or three are gathered in my name...' and John 17:20 'that they all may be one'. That was his greatest concern; his desire that there should be unanimity of understanding and feeling between clergy and laity, and he believed that the liturgy could bring that about.

If however this was to be achieved, the people must be instructed in the mysteries underlying the liturgy, and in the prayers, symbols and actions of the Mass and of course of other parts of the liturgy. In this context he repeats his teaching about response: 'Christ and his church have instituted divine worship, composed of words and meaningful signs, for the Christian people, in order that they may respond and take an active part in it' (This again sounds very much like the Constitution on the Liturgy). But, insists Rosmini, the instruction must not be formulas learnt by heart. Experience shows, he says, that the recitation of catechism formulas is inadequate. They are dead words and need to be brought alive. The instruction must be 'full

and living', leading ultimately to life. Again, this is an anticipation of modern catechetics.

Unless and until this is done the people 'have scarcely a material
presence at worship' for 'it is very difficult for civilised people to
be present at rites which they neither understand or share'. They
are like 'statues and pillars'.

Did then Rosmini go as far as asking for the use of the people's
language in the liturgy? Perhaps on account of the very conservative attitudes in Rome and elsewhere at the time he rejected the
notion of translating the liturgy and he rehearses all the arguments against it which had been ventilated in the eighteenth
century, arguments that were current until Vatican II. For him
the problems raised would be greater than the benefits of the
remedy. He concludes by setting out four requirements:

1. The study of Latin should be promoted among the laity,
using modern methods (i.e. not just the old grind of much
grammar and not much else).

2. There should be thorough instruction (in the sense already
defined) in the meaning of the liturgy (it is doubtful whether
this has been done in our own time).

3. Books should be provided for the laity with translation of
the texts of the missal, etc. (This has been done on a great scale
in the last hundred years or more and England was a leader in
doing so. See John Goter's translation of the Roman Missal
which appeared in 1718).

4. It is the duty of the clergy to promote these matters. But
since he had a low view of the education of the clergy he cannot have been very hopeful. The inadequacies of the education
of the clergy is the next 'Wound'.

Limited as Rosmini's remedies may be thought to be, by 1832 he
had come to a viewpoint very like that of Dom Lambert
Beauduin who in 1909 inaugurated the pastoral movement of
which the Second Vatican Council was the fruit. It is hazardous
to speculate on what Rosmini would have thought or done if he
had lived in this century but he is in the honourable succession
of the now canonised Giuseppe Tommasi and Muratori, and
with them can be counted as a forerunner of the modern liturgical movement.

(The quotations in the above article are taken, with permission, from *The Five Wounds of the Church*, translated from the critical edition *Delle cinque Piaghe della Santa Chiesa*, Citta Nuova, Rome, 1981, by Fr Denis Cleary (Fowler Wright Books, Leominster, 1987).

A biographical note on Rosmini

He was born in 1797 at Rovereto of a noble family. After studies at Padua he was ordained priest in 1821. With the encouragement of Popes Pius VIII and Gregory XVI, he undertook a renewal of Italian philosophy (including St Thomas Aquinas). He was a philosopher of great depth but some of his theological views (e.g. on transubstantiation) were condemned as unorthodox. His attack on Probabilism annoyed the Jesuits and he was accused of Jansenism and pantheistic tendencies. In 1828 he had founded the 'Fathers of Charity', usually known in this country as Rosminians. From 1850 he led a retired life in north Italy until his death in 1855.

See account in the *Oxford Dictionary of the Christian Church* (2nd rev. ed. 1983) s.v. 'Rosmini-Serbati'.

Notes

1. It was to be found on the shelves of the library at Oscott College in an English translation where I first saw it over sixty years ago.

2. See Cattaneo, *Il Culto...*', p 561 (the brackets are mine).

3. *Summa Theol.* pt III, Q 63, aa 2–6.

CHAPTER IV

Liturgical Reform
from a Tainted Source
The Synod of Pistoia (1786)

The Synod of Pistoia, which was convened by Scipio de' Ricci, bishop of that place with Prato, in conjunction with Leopold the Grand Duke of Tuscany and brother of Joseph II, Emperor of the Austro-Hungarian empire, was influenced by Gallicanism, Jansensim and the Enlightenment as operated in his realm by Joseph II. The Synod accepted the famous Gallican statement of the French Church of 1682 which severely limited the role and action of the pope in the affairs of the church in France. From the Jansenists it took their doctrine of grace and predestination, on the sacrament of Penance (rejecting attrition or sorrow born of fear) and, as we shall see, much of their views on liturgical practice. The Enlightenment is represented by the Josephite attack on devotions, the rejection of pilgrimage, praying before statues and the attempt to evacuate religious worship, whether public or private, of any warmth. Enthusiasm was anathema.

Here we are concerned only with propositions about liturgical reform which in fact do not show any very great originality, at least to those familiar with the French scene of the previous century.

Like the Jansenists, Ricci wanted to cut out the Middle Ages which to him were barbarous, but more importantly, it was the time of the Scholastic theology with its complications, and distinctions and the whole apparatus of its dialectic which had seriously damaged the pure and clear (?) doctrine of the Fathers of the Church. The advance of patristic and liturgical knowledge made in the seventeenth and eighteenth centuries had also revealed a simpler and more accessible style of worship, contrasted with which the Jansenists and Ricci found the current rite over-elaborate, pompous and remote from the people, large numbers of whom were illiterate. Ricci, again like *some* of the Jansenists, would go back to basics.

Had the laity any role except watching and listening in the celebration of the liturgy, and if so what was it based on? Ricci in his
Synod brought back the doctrine of the priesthood that the baptised Christians share with Christ. By reason of this 'they can
and should offer spiritual sacrifices of praise and thanksgiving
to God, and because, even though all do not consecrate the Body
and Blood of Jesus Christ in the visible sacrifice of the altar, yet
all who take part in it offer the spotless Lamb'.[1] There was the
desire to restore the liturgy as 'an action common to people and
priest' (p 82). One way of achieving this would be 'through
greater simplicity of rites, by expounding it (the liturgy) in the
language of the people and by pronouncing it in a clear voice'
(p 82). There was also a reference to Canon of the Mass and how
the priest should 'pronounce all the words distinctly and devoutly'
and that there was to be no organ music from the offertory to the
postcommunion prayer.[2] This seems to suggest that the Canon
should be pronounced aloud, in a voice that could be heard by
all, a practice not unknown in France in Jansenising circles. It
was done by the parish priest of Asniéres with the astonishing
name of Jubé (which means 'rood-screen'). He said the Canon so
that all could hear it and, in addition, he sang the Kyrie, the
Gloria, the Sanctus and the Credo with the people, and listened
to the epistle and gospel as they were sung by assistant ministers.[3]

There was to be only one altar in each church, as in ancient
times, as this would facilitate the gathering of the people round
the altar and eliminate the practice of quasi-private Masses said
in side-chapels while the principal Mass was being said. There
must be no flowers or relics on the altar; the latter, if authentic,
might be placed under it (as is now ordered by the Rite of
Dedication of Altars!). Holy Communion should be received at
Mass as it is 'an *essential*' part of it. Theologians would say that it
is an *integral* part. And communion should be given from bread
consecrated at the Mass the people attended; this in accordance
with the ruling of Benedict XIV.

As for reservation of the Blessed Sacrament, it should be in the
most prominent place and this in the mind of the Synod (or
Ricci!) was *above* the High Altar. It was to be suspended in a kind
of ciborium (in the form of a dove?), as indeed it had been at Port
Royal.

People were to be urged to take part in the Divine Office, especially on Sundays and feast days and to this end the Breviary must be reformed and simplified, and a new kind of book was to be prepared containing the offices of Sundays and feasts, psalms and hymns to be in Italian, and a translation of the Ordinary of the Mass.[4]

The purpose of al these suggested regulations was that people should have easier access to the Mass and other rites, so that they could understand them better and in some sense participate. It is not clear however whether all or any of these regulations were put into practice, least of all one that urged that if the liturgy were in the language of the people, it would be easier for them to join their voices with that of the Church.[5]

There were criticisms of other current practices, notably concerning the sacrament of Penance. The French Jansenists had a strong desire to return to the ancient discipline of penance of the fourth/fifth centuries. They realised however that was impossible so they made much of the need for true repentance to be manifested by external signs (fasting and works of mercy) before absolution should be given. There are reflections of this way of thinking in the proceedings of the Synod. There was admiration for the old discipline, penitential works before absolution and the importance of prayer in the celebration of the sacrament was emphasised. Accordingly there was criticism of those priests who used *only* the formula of absolution, *Ego te absolv*o. (Bolton, p 86).

Information about the Anointing of the Sick was for its time correct enough but it was almost certainly derived from the Jansenising and very rigorous Bishop of Aleth of the seventeenth century. The Synod observed that the Anointing, then called Extreme Unction, was neglected because it had become associated with the death bed. Likewise, it was an error to treat it as the *last* sacrament. The Last Sacrament is holy communion in the form of Viaticum (again something that has been made clear by Vatican II).

Like Muratori, but in a much more dictatorial way, the Synod was severely critical of the plethora of devotional practices some of which the members of the Synod thought were tinged with superstition and in any case drew people away from what was essential. Religious pictures in church that suggested pomp and vanity were to be removed (one supposes they were those late and elaborate baroque pictures which were no longer in the taste of the time), images in which people seemed to have a special 'faith', those under a special title (Our Lady of this or that place or 'virtue'), should be abolished and the practice of clothing statues should cease. Images and devotions that suggested false doctrines must also go (Denz. 1569). One of these was devotion to the Sacred Heart of Jesus. Although the Jansenists of the seventeenth century had accepted the devotion, those of the eighteenth contemptuously rejected it, calling its devotees *'cordicoles'*, heart worshippers. This view appears in the Synod proceedings. Worship of the Sacred Heart was reprehensible because worship of a human organ was idolatry. The Synod saw it as the worship of the human heart of Jesus as *separated* from his divinity. Rome, in the *Auctorem fidei* of 1794, had to point out that the humanity of Christ is inseparably united to the divinity.

There were other matters that concerned the Synod. It urged that the laity must read and be allowed to read the Bible and only 'real inability' to do so (presumably illiteracy or blindness) could excuse them. The Synod thus deliberately repeated a proposition of Paschase Quesnel which had been condemned by the Bull *Unigenitus* of 1713. Rome condemned it once more (Denz. 1567). The Roman view was that the Bible reading was good (though the officials of the Curia do not seem to have been keen on it) but not necessary for salvation, as at least some Jansenists averred. Bibles may be read but only in translations authorised by bishops and they must include annotations and explanations warning against heterodox understandings of the text.

If it is asked what effect the Synod of Pistoia had, the answer is that from one point of view practically none and from another point of view nothing but calamity. The Grand Duke wanted to call a National Council of the bishops of Tuscany, Ricci was reluctant and the duke contented himself with calling an assembly of bishops of Florence. Not all came and those who did showed differences of opinion, especially on the subject of obedience to the Apostolic See whose authority was obviously going to be flouted. Then rumours had been circulating in Prato for some time that the altar of 'Our Lady's Girdle' in the cathedral was to be destroyed. Other changes had been made there too and the people had had enough. They rose up in tumult. What had been taken out of the cathedral was put back and there was much burning of various items. Troops had to be called in to restore peace. The *Acts* of the Synod were, against the wishes of Ricci, published in 1788, and whether *post hoc propter hoc*, a riot broke out in Pistoia. Ricci fled and in 1791 he resigned his bishopric. The people rejected Ricci's benevolent attempts to improve their spiritual lot, as did the people in Austria.

Meanwhile there was no reaction from Rome. Leopold had succeeded his brother Joseph II in 1790 and for various reasons Pius VI did not want to jeopardise his relations with him. It was not until 1794 that the Constitution *Auctorem fidei* appeared when much of Europe had other things to think about (the French Revolution). It was largely concerned with authority and Jansenism. The Synod had deliberately and knowingly attempted to usurp the supreme authority of the Apostolic See and the pope condemned its proceedings on this account as schismatical. Secondly, the pope condemned all the propositions that sought to authenticate the often condemned teaching of the Jansenists. These were condemned as heretical. Other matters with which we have been concerned here were condemned in various tones of voice, so to say. They were 'temerarious', or 'against the customs of the Church', or 'as understood' (*sic intellecta*), or as the 'underlying doctrine insinuates' (*quatenus insinuat doctrina*) and so on. So such notions as that there should be only one altar in the church or that the language of the people might be used or that the people should take an active part in the Mass were rejected not in themselves but on account of the context in which they were set.[6] The important point of these perhaps tedious details is that the Church did not wish to commit itself definitely on these issues which were beyond the competence of a local synod. This did not exclude the possibility of their implementation at some future date though it is likely that the authorities thought that date would never come. It is curious that, as far as I am aware, during the often angry controversy over the 'changes in the liturgy' after the Second Vatican Council no one brought up the condemnations of the *Auctorum fidei* as marks of the inconsistency of the Church's policy in these matters. Perhaps it was a sign that the Synod of Pistoia was truly dead and buried.

What seems to be a just summing up of Ricci and his work is to be found in the *Enciclopedia Italiana*: '...at a time of laxity among the clergy, of clerical ignorance, of superstition among the people, and of an increasing tide of religious indifference and atheistic rationalism, Ricci dreamed of and willed, in spite of many errors, a learned and disinterested clergy and a fervent and devoted people. Yet by his reforms he ended up by drifting towards heresy and schism, and through his political attitude he came to subject the interests of the Church to those of the State'.[7]

Bibliography

C. A. Bolton's *Church Reform – The Synod of Pistoia* (see n 1) is an excellent account of the Synod and its preparation and consequences. E. Cattaneo *Il Culto in Occidente* cites certain texts not to be found in Bolton. Owen Chadwick gives a clear account in *The Popes and the European Revolution* (1981), pp 424-431.

The Edition used of Denzinger *Enchiridion Symbolorum...* is the 17th (1928), the numbers referring to Pistoia are 1501–1599. These will be different in later editions.

Notes

1. See for this and all the following quotations Charles A. Bolton, *Church Reform in 18th century Italy* (The Synod of Pistoia) Martinus Nijhoff, the Hague, 1969, p 79.

2. Op cit, p 82.

3. See L. Bouyer, *Liturgical Piety* (Notre Dame Press, Indiana, 1955) p 53.

4. See Cattaneo, *Il Culto...*, pp 524, 527, 528.

5. cf. Denzinger, 1566.

6. See my 'Historical Sketch of the Roman Liturgy' in *True Worship*, ed. Lancelot Sheppard (Darton, Longman and Todd, 1963) p 79, n 3. J. A. Jungmann took the same view.

7. Quoted in C. A. Bolton, *Church Reform ...*', p 129.

CHAPTER V

The German Scene

To be exact one would have to say 'the scene in the Germanys' which, apart from the Austro-Hungarian Empire, consisted of numerous duchies and princedoms, some Catholic and some Protestant. Until the rise of Frederick the Great of Prussia, the Austro-Hungarian Empire dominated much of southern and central Europe reaching out to Hungary and to what until recently was called Czechoslovakia. From a religious and liturgical point of view this was important as those regions, as well as almost the whole of northern Italy, were under the influence of the Austrian, i.e. the Habsburg, monarchs. What they decreed affected vast areas of Europe.

It was the age of the Benevolent Despot who were often more despotic than benevolent. Some at least had every intention of making the Church a department of state and they interfered in the affairs of the Church from the effective appointment of bishops to the way people should say their prayers and worship God. Even the Empress Maria Theresa, devout Catholic though she was, dealt with popes and bishops to suit herself and in some ways prepared the way for the 'reforms' of her son, Joseph II.

The eighteenth century was, as everyone knows, the age of the Enlightenment or the *Aufklärung* which dominated the whole of western Europe and, through Catherine the Great, made its way into Russia. It was an age that was unpropitious for Christian faith and worship. It rejected everything that went beyond the criteria of its narrow and shallow rationalism. On these terms Christianity was intellectually untenable. It claimed to be a religion based on a revelation coming from another world. This and faith in a personal God, in the divinity of Christ and his resurrection, the infallibility of the Bible and the divine origin of the Church as well as miracles were all rejected. The Deists, so numerous at the time, admitted the existence of a God who had set the world in motion but now he was the Great Unemployed. A church that could teach and celebrate mysteries beyond the proof of reason or the empirical sciences was ridiculous and can be said to have evoked Voltaire's '*Écrasez l'infâme*' even though he professed belief in some sort of God.

There was resistance from the Church and its clergy in both France and the Germanys but the theological level of the time was low; no great minds appeared able to tackle the acute problems raised by the philosophers and others who dominated the intellectual world. It is understandable, then, that priests and even professors of theology should have been affected by the spirit of the time. They tended to soft-pedal the mystery element in the Christian religion and laid great stress on 'catechism' and moral instruction, both good things in themselves, but they were given in a dry and formal fashion. Such instruction did not engage the affections or the sentiments of the hearers. For the young it was also compulsory (the hour for giving it was 1.00 pm on a Sunday!) and so was not likely to be popular.

All this broadly speaking was the spirit of the times, the *Zeitgeist*, and however regrettable it was, it is not surprising that the clergy were influenced by it. The Latin Mass, as it was, was a highly complicated rite; the celebrant had his back to the people, he did mysterious things over the bread and the chalice, the chants overlapped what he doing, the Sanctus for instance continued while the first part of the Canon of the Mass was being said (of course silently) and the only text read in the vernacular was the gospel, and that by no means everywhere. A great deal of clutter had been imposed on the rite of the Mass and in their efforts to get rid of it the clergy were in danger of turning the Mass into something merely didactic. The Mass came to be looked upon as an exercise in moral uplift.

Yet not all their notions were wrong. Many saw that the Mass was the action not just of the priest but of the assembled community and this here and there they tried to emphasise; the people should attend the Mass in their parish church (and not at shrine-chapels or those of religious), the principal Mass should be celebrated without the distraction of 'private' Masses in side-chapels, the sermon must take place after the gospel (and not *after* Mass), and the people should be able to receive communion

after the priest and not after Mass or at some other time. Those
who wanted but one Mass on Sunday said that there should be
only one altar and seem to have been extremists like Scipio de'
Ricci of Pistoia.

Out of this understanding of the rite of the Mass came the teaching that the people should follow the action of the Mass and not
have recourse to private prayers and devotions. How was this to
be done? There were those who wished to re-activate the offertory procession (long obsolete) as this would give the people
some visible part of the celebration. To this they would have
added the revival of the giving of the peace (which survived at
the High Mass but only among the clergy!). There were even
some who wanted to restore concelebration as a way of getting
rid of the multiplicity of Masses in side-chapels. As J. A.
Jungmann[1] remarks, whatever else may be thought of all this, it
bears witness to the pastoral sense of the clergy. Of course it was
all unlawful; as Rome made emphatically clear in the *Auctorem
fidei*, local bishops or episcopates had no authority to make
changes in the liturgy. But, as far as the clergy were concerned, it
was the age of Febronianism which was a German form of
Gallicanism, and bishops in their view *did* have the authority to
do what was suggested and sometimes put into practice.

Given this understanding of the situation the further question
was how it could be achieved? In Germany, since the later
Middle Ages, there had been a practice of interpolating German
verses into some of the Latin texts of the Mass (rather like the
macaronic English carols). Into the Sequences (many at the time)
were inserted German verses between Latin ones, and songs
(*Gesänge*) were sung before and after the sermon which of course
may have been preached after the Mass (as was long the custom)
or on another occasion altogether. But since the number of
Sequences was severely reduced in the Pius V Missal, the custom of singing German during the liturgy began to die. Yet always, alongside the Catholics, was the Lutheran church with its
great tradition of hymns (some of which had their origin in the
Middle Ages) and musical giants like John Sebastian Bach. This
tradition acted in two ways, by attraction and repulsion.
Conventional Catholics thought it wrong to copy the Lutherans
and to sing German hymns during or in connection with the
liturgy; others thought it right to learn from the Protestants and

no doubt it was these who kept alive or revived the practice of singing in German in Catholic churches. A different influence came from the *Aufklärung*. As we have seen, everything had to be plain and intelligible. The Mass and other parts of the liturgy must be understandable and if the people were to follow the action of the Mass, they must be helped to do so. It was, then, in this eighteenth century that the tradition of some German in the Mass was revived. The device used for the Mass was to compose German texts with music that should accompany the parts of the Mass that were to be sung by the people: the Kyrie, the Gloria, the Creed, the Sanctus and the Agnus Dei and even, it seems, there were texts corresponding to the 'propers' of the Sunday or feast day. The priest of course was required to say in Latin the texts sung in German by the people, though one wonders whether he always did so.

The first beginnings may not have been altogether satisfactory, some of the texts were banal, the verses pedestrian and even bathetic but it was a developing process and came to be established under the name of the *Betsingmesse* (lit. the prayer-sing-mass) which met the needs of the people up to this century. There was also a gradual improvement of the rite and the name changed to the *Deutsches Hochamt* (German High Mass).[2] It was much promoted by the excellent *Gesang-Bücher* which, though diocesan in principle, contained the German Mass texts (and in fact other songs) that were common to all. It should be noted that these books always retained some of the familiar Latin texts which were sung according to the Gregorian melodies.

There was one defect in this form of celebration: there was no dialogue between the priest and the people. The collects, the epistle (the gospel will have been sung in Latin and then repeated in German), the preface and the Pater noster remained in Latin which last the people could have sung with the priest, but it was not allowed. Somewhat like other attempts to bring the people closer to the Mass, it remained a parallel liturgy rather than the direct celebration of the liturgy by the people.

The development of the *Betsingmesse*, which is recorded as early as 1726, seems to have been gradual and since it was promoted by the clergy (and not by the emperor), it was widely accepted and seems to have caused no upset. Not so the ruthless reforms which the Emperor Joseph II tried to impose on his people. The people's reaction in Italy to the attempted reforms encapsulated in the Synod of Pistoia has already been mentioned. If reactions in the vast territories of the emperor were less violent they were no more favourable. As soon as the people got the chance, they returned to their old ways.

Much has already been said about the Josephite ideas but a few examples of his interference in public worship will illustrate the extent of the invasion of the secular power into the most intimate details of worship.

In all parish churches on Sundays and feasts of obligation, there should be a sermon at an early hour for those in service (but no Mass at this hour apparently). There must be another sermon at a later hour for the rest of the parishioners.

On workdays there was to be one Mass and 'Benediction with the ciborium', though the regulation does not say when this service was to take place. Benediction with chants accompanied by the organ was to be given with the monstrance. On Sundays and feast days there was to be but one Mass with instrumental music; lacking that there were to be 'choral chants' – whatever that may mean.

On Sunday afternoons there was to be Catechism or 'Christian doctrine', so given as to instruct the adults as well as the young. This was part of all the didactic emphasis of the time.

In public churches there was to be daily the Litany of Saints, said 'in a loud voice' with the usual prayers, including the one for the sovereign.

In the evening there were also to be public prayers daily. These prayers morning and evening were intended to eliminate novenas, popular prayers to our Lady and the saints and other devotional practices (like the lighting of candles) to which the people were so attached.[3]

These regulations were only part of the Josephite reforms and what the people thought of them is not easy to describe. That they heartily disliked them is certain and there was much muttering in dark corners. In any case Joseph did not win. When he and his successors were swept away, the people returned to their old devotions.

The introduction of German chants into the Mass seems to have satisfied the majority though a certain affection and concern for Latin remained. The German texts were often prosaic and the more conservative thought the translation of the whole Mass would be similar. There was also hesitance about seemingly to 'go Protestant'. On the other side, there were those who rehearsed the arguments for the vernacular with which we became very familiar before Vatican II: priest and people should be able to worship as a community, the people responding to and offering with the priest, the need to understand, for *all* to understand, though some of the less educated or perhaps those who did not know German very well did not welcome the use of the vernacular. The movement towards it however, became strong, the influence of the Enlightenment was still powerful. The first Mass in German was translated by Father Benedikt Werkmeister, a Benedictine, and was celebrated by him in 1786 in the private chapel of the Palace of Stuttgart. The Canon of the Mass however remained in Latin! Perhaps it was thought that even in German the Canon would not be very intelligible, or more likely, it was an attachment to tradition. In any case he hoped his translation and practice would be a model for others to copy.

After the formal end of the Holy Roman Empire, forced on Austria by Napoleon in 1806, there was a further phase of secularisation. Monasteries were closed or combined, religious houses of women emptied, religious sisters diverted to 'useful' work, and there was the now rather stale attack on 'superstition' among the peasants, prohibition of devotional practices like pilgrimages, the reduction of saints' days and so on. To supervise this revolution a church committee was set up of which Benedikt Werkmeister, now an ex-Benedictine, was chairman. His deplorable actions in the sphere of the religious orders and houses do not concern us here but it was in this context that there emerged a Breviary in German. It appeared in the diocese of Augsburg, translated by an orientalist, and offered to the clergy and nuns and to 'any good Christians'. It was taken up by the Elector of Cologne, by Augsburg itself, by Würzburg and went into eight editions (1810–1821). Although omitting traditional material like responses, antiphons and hymns, and reducing the number of psalms to be said to eighty, it proved to be very popular. Its comparatively long life is proof of that.[4]

If we are to judge the German liturgical reforms we need to put them in context. Their promoters were undoubtedly under the influence of the *Aufklärung* which, if often narrowly rationalistic, also opened people's eyes to matters that had for long been taken for granted. It promoted liberty of thought (which of course could be abused just as repression of thought is an abuse), it made people review their situations (the *Aufklärung* eventually brought political freedom), and to examine their religious habits and practices. The rite of the Roman Mass looked to many to be an archaeological remain, complicated and unintelligible to people most of whom had little or no education. What the priest did at the altar seemed infinitely remote from the people who had little part in it. It was celebrated in a language they could not understand and often there was no sermon. The clergy, if influenced by the *Aufklärung*, had their eyes opened to pastoral needs and they sought ways of meeting them. Hence, among other things, the *Betsingmesse* which in fact endured even if it had to be revised and improved as time went on. On the other hand efforts to turn the rite of the Mass and the Divine Office into German had no long-lasting effect.

Then there was the question of legality. Had bishops and priests the authority to make the changes? By Roman standards no, but throughout the eighteenth century the papacy was weak and without prestige, except for Benedict XIV who could reach out to such a one as Voltaire, and Ganganelli, Clement XIV, who has earned a lasting notoriety as the pope who suppressed the Jesuits. Faced with the unbenevolent despots who dominated the life of the church in their territories, the popes found no way of resisting their incursions into church affairs. In these circumstances there developed what has been called episcopalism. In France, the Germanys and Spain the monarch nominated bishops who by consequence were beholden to those to whom they owed their jobs. Recourse to Rome was hindered and so they decided to act *motu proprio* in liturgical and other matters. They accepted what pastoral priests put before them or allowed it to go ahead. It was not until the prestige and the papacy had risen, as it did in the nineteenth century and especially in the second half, that private enterprise in liturgy was brought to an end.

If it be asked what of this effort towards liturgical reform remained, the answer must be that the German-speaking peoples
had for generations the lived experience of worshipping in their
own language, even if only in a limited way, and that they were
ready for a vernacular liturgy when it came.

Notes

1. *Missarum Sollemnia, I* (French trans. 1950), pt 1, ch 13, pp 182ff.
ET *The Mass of the Roman Rite*, Vol 1, ch 13, (New York, 1951,
1955).

2. See J. A. Jungmann *Liturgisches Erbe and Pastorale Gegenwart*
(1960), p 453; ET, *Pastoral Liturgy* (London, 1962), pp 346–7. As
late as 1943 the texts were brought closer to the Latin and, as I
was told years ago, this was a great improvement. The
Betsingmesse attracted a good deal of attention outside German-
speaking lands and prepared the way for the liturgical reforms
of Vatican II.

3. See Cattaneo, *Il Culto in Occidente*, pp 505-515.

4. See O. Chadwick, *The Popes and European Revolution*, pp 439-
443; 504-508.

CHAPTER VI

The 'Neo-Gallican' Books

When most modern Christians are confronted with the phenom-
enon of the revision of the liturgical books in eighteenth century
France they are usually somewhat puzzled. Had not the Council
of Trent decreed a revision of the Roman rite and committed the
work to the pope? And had he not laid down that the whole of
the Church in the west (which would include the New World)
should follow and use the Roman books and those only. Local
churches like Milan with its Ambrosian rite, and religious orders
like the Dominicans who could claim two hundred years of
existence for their liturgies, were indeed exempted but only
those. What right then had the Church in France to revise the
liturgical books without a by-your-leave to Rome? The answer
raises the whole question of Gallicanism. The Church in France
claimed what it called 'Gallicanism liberties' which according to
the French were centuries old. While maintaining union with
Rome and recognising the pope as the (earthly) head of the
Church the bishops, backed by the king, insisted on their right to
conduct their own affairs while having recourse to Rome only in
matters of faith. Recourse to Rome in the seventeenth century
was in fact quite frequent over the heresy of Jansenism, even
Louis XIV finding it useful and necessary if he was to have his
way with the Jansenists. Rome never recognised the 'Gallican
liberties', nor did the pope endorse the new-Gallican revisions
of the liturgical books but it is strange that, as far as this writer
knows, Rome never condemned these books or forbade their
use.[1a]

Modern French liturgical scholars have questioned the accuracy
of the term 'Neo-Gallican', used early in this century by Abbot
Fernand Cabrol and Dom Henry Leclercq, editors of the vast
Dictionnaire d'Archéologie chrétienne et de Liturgie.[1] The term is unsatisfactory because first, it gives the impression that the French

Church was attempting to restore the ancient Gallican liturgy in use in Gaul up to the eighth century, and secondly, that there was a wholesale re-writing of the Roman books. This was not so. As Pierre Jounel makes clear, the *Ordo Missae* and the Canon of the Roman Missal were always preserved, with one or two exceptions as to the former. The first revised Gallican missal appeared in 1685 and to it were added scripture readings for the Wednesdays and Fridays of every week. This, says Jounel, was rather a happy addition to the Lectionary than a revolution.[2] These had indeed been taken from the ancient *Ordo Lectionum* of the ninth century and had been in use until the reform of the Roman rite in the sixteenth century. A similar Lectionary is to be found in the Sarum Missal, widely in use in England before the Reformation. It seems that whether formally or informally, the French bishops were appealing to the two hundred year rule to justify their actions. This would seem to be true also for the replacement of some of the collects of the Roman Missal by others, thought more suitable, from ancient sources, including those regarded as Roman, the Gelasian and the Leonine. Where, quite deliberately, they diverged from the Roman tradition was in the substitution of texts of the chants with new ones, e.g. the introits. They did this for two reasons. They rejected on principle any chant-texts that were not to be found in the scriptures, like the *Gaudeamus omnes in Domino* which was the introit for certain feasts. Secondly, some revisers developed what must be called 'theme' Masses. Sometimes they would take the theme of the gospel of the day and make the (new) introit and the collect conform to it. Where possible they brought in also the epistle and the gradual that followed it. These 'themes' are described as largely moralising, directed first to the clergy and through them to the people in the hope that the clergy would teach (in homilies and sermons no doubt) what they celebrated in the liturgy. The danger was that the liturgy became a didactic tool rather than the celebration of the central mysteries of the faith, the life, passion, death and resurrection of Christ. This was all in accord with the spirit of the time, the Enlightenment, that consciously or unconsciously affected the revisers and the bishops who prompted, sanctioned and published their new missals.

Before considering a small selection of these missals it is necessary to explain that the impetus for revision came from a dissatisfaction with the Breviary of 1568. This had imposed on the secular clergy a highly monastic office. There were on Sundays eighteen psalms in 'Mattins' and seven in Lauds or morning prayer proper (the last two were usually joined together in celebration). On the ferias (non-feast days) in 'Mattins' there were twelve psalms. The clergy naturally felt that all this was burdensome and thanks to a defective rubrical system which allowed for the celebration of saints' feasts that ousted the Sunday or ferial office they usually chose these feasts when the office was shorter. This was greatly to the detriment of the 'Green' Sundays after Pentecost and even to those of Lent when certain devotional Masses, largely concerned with the Instruments of the Passion, could be said instead of the ferial Mass and office. This system (if such it can be called) lasted until the reform of the Divine Office and calendar in 1912.

The first attempt at the reform of the Breviary came in 1670 when the Archbishop of Paris, Hardouin de Péréfixe, set up a commission. This decided that there should be no more than nine psalms at 'Mattins' (as in the Roman Breviary of 1912), that there should be a better choice of scriptural and patristic readings and that the would-be historical accounts of saints, which had long been a scandal to scholars, should be revised to accord with the canons of scholarship in the matter. It was this re-arrangement of the office that led to the first revision of the missal of Paris initiated by Hardouin de Péréfixe and after his death promulgated by his successor, François de Harlay de Champvallon in 1785. These changes in the Breviary required changes in certain elements of the missal, for example the calendar, and additions to the lectionary suggested similar treatment, for the missal. Restricted in the 1785 missal, this was carried through more extensively in later revised missals. Other additions were the composition of sequences for the missal and hymns (replacing the medieval ones) for the breviary. The liturgical books *looked* much the same and they were very well produced but all the same there was a subtle change of atmosphere. They were much plainer, stream-lined, and much of the ancient and perhaps untidy material had been removed.

The number of these French missals (with which usually went revisions of the breviary) is very great. Over a hundred have been listed (it is agreed that the lists are not complete) and were in use in 139 dioceses by 1790 when the French Revolution swept everything away. However, some of these books went on being used until 1850. After the Concordat with Napoleon in 1801 there were some seven or nine different breviaries being used in the diocese of Versailles and Beauvais.[3] It was this Augean liturgical stable that later on the Abbé Guéranger was determined to clear out.

One of earliest revised missals was that of the diocese of Meaux of which the bishop was the famous Jacques Bénigne Bossuet (+1704). Even during his life-time preparations were made for the revision of the liturgical books. As is well known, Bossuet was involved in early efforts of ecumenism and had conversations and correspondence with Archbishop Wake, with Leibniz and a Lutheran theologian Gerard Walter, alias Molanus. Writing to him Bossuet thus expressed his views about the revision of the books that had already taken place:

> 'The public prayers, the missals, the rituals, the breviaries, will be put in better form, after the example of those of the churches of Paris, Reims, Vienne, La Rochelle and other very illustrious (churches), such as the arch-monastery of Cluny and the whole of its (Benedictine) Order. Anything that is doubtful, suspect, apocryphal, or superstitious will be removed. All will be redolent of the piety of former times (*l'ancienne piété*)'. This very well expresses the spirit of the whole reform.

The work was put in hand only shortly after the death of Bossuet and the new bishop, Bissy, entrusted it to Francois Ledieu who had been secretary to Bossuet. His missal depended on that of Paris in the edition of the Cardinal de Noailles with 'some usages of the diocese of Meaux'; it seems to have been a conservative revision except for one feature. Very audaciously Ledieu directed that the Canon of the Mass should be said aloud, that the people should say Amen after the words of consecration and by placing R before the many Amens that then existed in the Canon he suggested that the people should say them. Ledieu introduced these outrageous directives as the book was going to the press and when it appeared it was immediately loudly and strongly criticised and had to be withdrawn.

The most radical, the most contentious and ultimately the most scandalous missal was that of the diocese of Troyes which appeared in 1736 in the pontificate of Jacques Benigne Bosuet, the

nephew of the great preacher. The king-pin of the commission
the bishop had set up was a Dr Nicolas Petitpied who had been
the leading spirit of the famous or infamous curé, Jubé of
Asnières, mentioned in a previous chapter of this book.[4] The
missal appeared in 1736 and caused scandal on account of the
following innovations.

1. The canon was to be said *submissiori voce* (not *secreto*), thus
suggesting that it should be recited so as to be heard by the congregation.
2. The rubric prescribing that the priest should recite privately
all that as said or sung by others was suppressed.
3. The Cross and candlesticks were not to be placed on the altar
(as at Asnières they were carried in and placed round the altar).
4. Prayers provided for the priest to be said before his communion
were suppressed.
5. Communion (of the people) must always be given during
Mass.

In addition, there were a great many more readings from the
scriptures; no text was to be read twice the same year. The book was
also more radical as it developed the theme Mass most rigorously:
in the Proper of Time there was one common theme built on the
collect, the epistle and the gospel, to which all the other texts
related.

The chapter of canons resisted as long as they could, no one
liked the book and in 1738 the metropolitan, Archbishop of Sens,
condemned all these innovations by order of the king.

The importance of the book is that, with the practices of the
parish of Asnières, it gave a model to Scipio de' Ricci and the
Synod of Pistoia.

The last missal we consider is that also called *Missale Parisiense*
but this one was edited at the direction of the Cardinal
Archbishop of Paris, glorying in name of Charles Gaspard
Guillaume Vintimille de Luc, and published in 1738. It had a
very wide circulation, being used in some fifty dioceses of
France. It was preceded by a breviary which was very radical
(the Offices of the last three days of Holy Week were completely
transformed) but the missal less so. It was based on the Paris
missal of 1785 which of course, like so many others, had been

edited by the committee of the Cardinal de Noailles, also Archbishop of Paris, a Janseniser. The committee consisted of Père Vigier, a French Oratorian, Philippe Mesenguy, an acolyte who was never ordained priest and was a Jansenist, condemned *nominatim* by the pope, and Charles Coffin, also a Jansenist and a hymnwriter. It was this collection of dubious characters that aroused the wrath and scorn of Abbot Guéranger when he came to write about the 'Neo-Gallican' liturgies in his *Institutions Liturgiques*. One priest, one acolyte and, Oh horror, one *layman*. This shocked Guéranger to the core.[5]

In the missal the lectionary and the collects of the Roman Missal were kept practically intact for Masses throughout the year and for the greater feasts. More changes were made in the prayers over the offerings and the post-communions and for the feasts of saints. For the 'Commons' the revisers drew on ancient sacramentaries such as the Gelasian and the Leonine (Verona), though there were new compositions also. The introits and other choral chants with texts drawn from the scriptures replaced the ancient but non-scriptural ones. The number of Prefaces was increased (following the pattern of the Gelasian Sacramentary), and among them were texts for Advent, Maundy Thursday, Corpus Christi and for many saints and the dead. Among the prefaces of Masses for the Dead was the one that now stands as number 1 in the Roman missal of 1970. It has sometimes been called 'Gallican' meaning 'Neo-Gallican' but it is in fact ancient and one would guess that it is the best liked of all in the present missal. Illogically, the revisers increased the number of those non-scriptural texts called sequences.

One reflection on all the liturgical revision is that it was a very clerical affair. It was directed to the clergy who would, it was thought, have a more streamlined and scriptural liturgy which they could more easily use for the instruction, i.e. moralisation of their people. The only book provided for the people; it seems, was the following: *Livre d'Eglise latin-français suivant les nouveaux Bréviaire et Missel de Paris ... à l'usage des laiques'*. It was published in 1772 and again in 1787. There were a number of *parossiens* in circulation but their content was very various and often the private prayers crowded out whatever liturgical texts were included. In short, this prolonged exercise in the revision of the liturgical books left the people very much where they were.[6]

Was all this effort in vain? The books at any rate survived the Revolution and some were being used until about 1850. Different missals, breviaries and rituals were being used in different dioceses and there was undoubtedly some confusion. The bishops of the Restoration were still largely Gallican in outlook and wanted things to go on much as before. The younger clergy were more ultramontane and some at least found a leader in the charismatic Félicité de Lamennais who managed to combine ultramontanism with democracy. He was in contact with the young Guéranger and for a short time influenced him. But when Lamennais became *more* interested in democracy than ultramontanism Guéranger would have no more to do with him. Guéranger in fact became ardently papal and anti-Gallican as well as fiercely anti-Jansenist. The 'Neo-Gallican' books had been the work of the Gallican bishops and their servants who included Jansenists, the sort known as the *'appelants'* who rejected the Bull *Unigenitus* which was the last condemnation of Jansenism, and the many propositions of Quesnel's *Moral Reflections on the New Testament*. To Guéranger's way of thinking the liturgical confusion reigning in France was a scandal and must be brought to an end. The Gallicanism and Jansenism that had produced the revised books were an even worse scandal. The bishops had arrogated to themselves the right of changing the liturgy, a right that was vested in the papacy alone. The Jansenists had insinuated their pernicious doctrines into the texts of the books though Guéranger was hard put to it to find them. All this irregular and heretical rubbish must be swept away and he would do the sweeping. This he did, conducting a veritable campaign, and did not stop at offending bishops and upsetting the clergy. Historians are agreed that the situation of the first half of the nineteenth century needed improving but they were also agreed that in his campaign Guéranger swept away many ancient and laudable customs that had belonged to the French church long before the reform of Pius V had taken place. For Guéranger the only *correct* rite was the Roman rite as he knew it, i.e. as revised in the sixteenth century (though he had to make exception for the monastic office which presumably he thought did not come under the same heading). He had a grudging attitude to the Ambrosian rite, he thought the suppression of the so-called the Mozarabic rite by the Benedictines and Gregory VII was a good thing, and he entertained the illusion that in the event of the reunion of the Eastern Churches with Rome their liturgies would die away to be replaced by that of Rome! All the same by about 1850 the liturgy in France had been 'romanised' though Gallican attitudes and anti-ultramontane attitudes, were detectable as late as the First Vatican Council in 1870.[7]

It could be said that there was one result of the neo-Gallican editors. The revisers of the Roman Missal of 1970 used a few of the collects that had appeared in their books. Hymns written by Santeul and Coffin appear in translation in various hymnals. Finally, the neo-Gallicans, whether orthodox or unorthodox, were good liturgical scholars.

Notes

1a. The pope condemned Vintimille's missal of 1738 but this was on account of its Jansenist connections. See *Anamnesis, Panorama Storico* 2, p 243 (Casale Monferrato) 1978. Benedict XIV is said to have admired the French liturgical books.

1. DACL tome 6, 1ère partie (1924) col 1875–1879; ibid, tome 9, 2è partie, (1930), col 1636-1729.

2. *La Maison-Dieu*, 141, (1980), p 94.

3. Rousseau, *Hist. du Mouvement Liturgique*, (Paris, 1945) p 28.

4. See p 31.

5. See *Institutions Liturgiques*. Extraits. Made by Jean Vaquié (Chire-en-Montreuil, 1977), pp 164–176.

6. For the foregoing information about the 'Neo-Gallican' books see *La Maison-Dieu*, no 141 (1980): 'Les Missels Diocésans Français du 18e Siècle' by Pierre Jounel, pp 91–96: 'Présentation des Missels Diocésans Français du 17e au 19e Siècle' by Gaston Fontaine, ibid pp 97-166.

7. For an account of Guéranger's campaign, which is quite balanced, see O. Rousseau, *Histoire...*, pp 25–43.

CHAPTER VII

Nicholas Le Tourneux (1640-1686)

Translator and Liturgist

The French church in the seventeenth century was a learned church. There were new editions of the Fathers, much interest in the early and medieval church (Le Nain de Tillemont, Mabillon) and, as has been shown in an earlier chapter, a deeper study of the liturgy and a desire to improve the current rite. Mabillon's editions of the *Ordines Romani* appeared after the death of Le Tourneux but they probably knew each other. Le Tourneux, who was learned, brought a different dimension to what may be called the seventeenth century liturgical movement. His dominant interest was what we now call pastoral liturgy. It was his great desire that the people should understand the liturgy and that they should take part in it so far as that was possible at the time. It was to facilitate this that he had the audacity to translate liturgical texts and on account of this he got into trouble with the church authorities of his time though his association with certain Jansenists made him vulnerable.

Born into a poor family at Rouen he early showed promise, and a benefactor, Thomas du Fossé (who was under Jansenist influence) became his patron and sent him to a Jesuit school in Paris. From there he passed to the Collège des Grassins for the arts course and philosophy. Instead, however, of embarking on the long course in theology at the Sorbonne, he went to the Touraine and studied theology with a parish priest. Ordained at the early age of 22 he was appointed to a working class parish in Rouen where his teaching of the young and his sermons attracted attention. He seems however to have been uncertain of himself, he had doubts about his ordination before the canonical age (though a dispensation had been granted) and, again with the help of the du Fossé family, got himself to Paris where he put off his clerical garb and wore grey. He came to know the Jansenists, Antoine Arnauld and Le Maitre de Saci who discerned in him gifts of which he was perhaps unaware.

They urged him to take up his duties again, a place as chaplain to the students at his old college was obtained and again his preaching and teaching were very successful. Also under Jansensist auspices, he was appointed Lent preacher at the church of St Benoit and had an enormous success. But he ran into trouble. The new archbishop of Parish, François de Harlay, more a politician than a priest, wanted him out of the way, there were charges of Jansenism which Louis XIV was determined to destroy, with the willing help of de Harlay. Le Tourneux decided to leave Paris and went to the little Priory at Villers-sur-Fère in Picardy, and there lived an austere life of prayer, public and private, self-denial and writing. He died of apoplexy in 1686.

Le Tourneux's contributions to pastoral liturgy are to be found in the following books:

De la meilleure manière d'entendre la Sainte Messe (1680).

Office de la Semaine Sainte, Latin et Français, à l'usage de Rome et du Paris, Avec explication des Cérémonies de l'Eglise... (1671, 1673).

Prières pour le Temps de l'avent appelées les O de Nöel selon le Bréviaire romain et... l'usage de Paris (s.d.)

L'Année chrétienne. Le Tourneux wrote this in the last years of his life but did not complete it. It is said that he completed only six volumes of the thirteen published. Other scholars say ten. However that may be, the additional volumes were written in the same style by Ruth d'Ans, a Belgian associated with the Jansenists.

The first book has a history. The archbishop of Rouen, the uncle of François de Harlay, Archbishop of Paris, had earlier in the century written a book for the people with a similar title. Le Tourneux, as he tells us, used this edition and adapted it to his own purposes.

Early in the book he states his purpose. According to the Council of Trent, he says, the people are to assist at Mass 'with sincere heart, a right faith, and reverent fear'. But there is another way, equally according to the mind of the Church and to the nature of the Mass itself. All (or almost all) the prayers of the Mass are in the plural and this is an indication that the people should join their hearts with the voice of the priest. Whether or nor Le Tourneux favoured *vocal* participation can be judged as we go through his commentary on the rite.

He seems to be envisaging a Low Mass in some places and a sung or High Mass in others. Thus, the Mass began in those days with the psalm 42 and of this Le Tourneux says that the priest recites it alternatively with the servers who represent the people because as Mgr Harlay has said, 'the people are clothed with the charity of the Church since they offer the sacrifice with him', i.e. the priest.

On the *Oremus* before the collect he instructs his readers to unite themselves with the prayer of the priest which they pray through him since he is praying in the name of the community.

When he comes to the offering or presentation of the bread and wine he has no doubt that this action belongs to the people:

'The offertory belongs more to the assistants (i.e. the people) than to the priest since it is an antiphon sung while he receives the offerings from the people. On the meaning of the action he writes much like modern liturgists: 'It is then the people who offer and *sing* while making their offering testify to the joy with which they present to God what they have received from him and which they will receive in turn at communion'. As we shall see, this practice survived in France at least on certain great feasts of the Church.

This was a gesture of active participation if ever there was one and Le Tourneux becomes even more explicit when he comes to comment on the *Orate, fratres*:

'(this invitatory) shows that the whole action of the Church is common to priest and people ... those who serve at the altar speak for all those present and it would be a good thing that all should know the response ... *to say it together*, or at least to unite their intention with that of the minister who serves the priest'.

Le Tourneux is evidently hesitant. He was no Jubé who would upset the whole world.

He knows however that there were certain abuses current that made the response to *Orate, fratres* impossible whether it was vocal or silent. He refers to those priests who during the Creed say the prayers of the offertory and do what is necessary then and thus deprive the people of their part: 'They (the priests) offer to God what they have not received ... (and) the people who *sing* the Creed cannot reply to the *Orate, fratres*'.

In his commentary on the Canon and the consecration he develops a theme that was common to him and other writers of the time. The consecration of the bread and wine does indeed belong to the priest exclusively but nonetheless what goes with it (he is thinking of the prayers before and after the consecration, especially the passage that begins *Unde et memores* where the 'holy people' are said to offer with the celebrant) is common to priest and people who if they are witnesses of the consecration yet offer the very body of Christ with the priest as (previously) they have made their offering of the bread. It is curious that he does not mention the wine in this place.

He was firm on the reception of holy communion during Mass and not after it: 'Nor should the priest and the people be separated at this time of the Mass any more than in the others; nor should they, without reason, receive communion afterwards for communion must be regarded as part of it', the Mass.

As we shall see, Goter's teaching in his *Instructions on Hearing Mass* is identical with Le Tourneux's and since there are certain verbal likenesses it seems certain that Goter knew his book.

As the title of the book *Office de la Semaine Saints* shows, it is a description of the Holy Week liturgy according to the usages of Rome and Paris. The latter should not surprise for, *pace* Abbot Guéranger, Paris like other great metropolitan sees had inherited these usages from the Middle Ages. Le Tourneux gives a lengthy commentary on the various rites, explains their meaning and provides a number of prayers. He seems to have liked writing prayers. It should also be noted that the book carries a translation from the Latin into French of the liturgical texts yet this particular book caused no furore at all.

In an introductory letter (addressed to 'Madame la Chancelière', the wife of Le Tellier, one of his patrons) he expounds the mean-

ing of Lent and Paschaltide. His source for the former is a homily
of St Leo the Great (+461) who wrote that though all times of the
year are dedicated to the service of God we should yet have a
special regard for Holy Week when we celebrate the principal
mysteries of faith. The Three Great Days, Maundy Thursday,
Good Friday and Easter 'present to us (*représent*) the mysteries
of the Passion and Resurrection of our Lord Jesus Christ which
the Church regards as the foundation of salvation'. Here he comes
very close to the modern theology of the presence of the mysteries
of salvation in and through the celebration of the liturgy.

Lent of course is a time of preparation for Holy Week, a time of
recollection when we withdraw from the world (a favourite
theme of the early Jansenists) and give ourselves to grateful
acknowledgement of God's graces; it is a time of purification of
heart 'to make us worthy to receive the fruits of the Passion and
Resurrection of Jesus Christ'. Lent too, according to St Augustine
(another source of his commentary), is a figure of this present
life which should be one of continual penitence. As for
Paschaltide it is obviously a time of rejoicing when the Christian
community 'seeks the things that are above' but it is also a symbol of the life to come when, with the saints, we shall be filled
with 'the eternal torrents of delight'. Lent enables us to enter
into a participation in the Passion and the cross so that 'we can
taste the fruits of Christ's Resurrection through the joy of
Paschaltide'. Evidently Le Tourneux had a unified view of Lent
and Easter and of Holy Week which, after St John Chrysostom,
he calls the Great Week. Le Tourneux was both patristic and
modern for all these ideas have been brought back in the last
fifty years.

Likewise in modern fashion he sees Lent and the liturgy of Holy
Week as the annual renewal of the Church and of the individual
Christian who if he/she is to celebrate the Paschal feast worthily
and be renewed in mind and heart must, with Jesus Christ and
like him, make the *passage* (cf John 13:1) from the old way of life
to the new. Symbols of the ritual renewal are the paschal fire, the
oils for baptism and confirmation, the water of baptism which
are all means to enable 'all members of the Church to participate
in the royal priesthood of her Bridegroom'.

But Le Tourneux was no ritualist. His abiding concern was that the celebration of the liturgy should be an exercise of mind and heart. Through the celebration of the liturgy the people will learn what should be 'the movements of the heart'. For – and this is a remarkable passage anticipating the future – the rites of the Church are intended to instruct the people through the eyes and teach them through the ear so that what they receive through the senses will enter their hearts. Seeing and hearing, both were important and the second was why Le Tourneux, even in the face of opposition, insisted on making translations of the liturgical texts. His concern was that what was celebrated externally should be interiorised and become part of the religion of the heart.

There was good reason for his concern, a concern St Vincent de Paul had earlier in the century. The manner of attending Mass at the time was very offhand. Even the literate took with them to church a 'book of hours' (i.e. the Little Office of the Blessed Virgin Mary) or some pious treatise such as the *Imitation of Christ*, they stood or knelt wherever they thought fit and gave their attention to the Mass only intermittently. Vast numbers made their Easter confession and communion and it was not only Jansenists who were concerned with their lack of preparation and devotion. It was Le Tourneux's hope that his books with their translations of the liturgical texts and their description of the rites would help people to take part in the liturgy with mind and heart.

The Romano-Paris liturgy of Holy Week was elaborate and from Le Tourneux's description very beautiful. It had more movement than the purely Roman rite and there was much in it to appeal to the eye and the ear. He is describing the cathedral liturgy but it was much the same in the many big churches of Paris where there were numerous staffs of priests and clerics who could undertake the liturgy in full. What the singing may have been is a matter for the musical experts but the texts sung by ministers were plainsong. The rest may have been characteristic of the *Grand siècle*.

Le Tourneux's description of the liturgy of Holy Week is very long and all we can do here is to select certain moments that have an interest of their own.

The Palm Sunday liturgy was very grand and recalls the rite as it is found in the Romano-German Pontifical of the tenth century from which the Roman rite was to obtain its rites. The liturgy began outside the church and there the palms were blessed, the people holding them in their hands (as now). The procession moved towards the church during the singing of five antiphons and when it came before a great cross a deacon sang the gospel of the palms (Matthew 21:1–9). Then followed a rite prevalent in the Middle Ages and found also in England: the cross was venerated and the ancient antiphon *Ave, Rex noster* (now restored to our rite) was sung. With the singing of five more antiphons the procession went to the church, the doors of which were shut. Clerics and choir boys inside the church sang the *Gloria laus* antiphonally with those outside, after which there was the opening of the doors. The celebrant (not the deacon or as formerly the subdeacon) struck the doors with the shaft of the processional cross three times while successively phrases from psalm 23 'Who is the King of glory' and the rest were sung. The doors were then opened and all entered the church to the singing of the *Ingrediente* and other chants.

One feature of the Maundy Thursday liturgy worth noting is that the Archbishop of Paris concelebrated the Mass with two senior canons. In the Church at the time it must have been a very rare practice.[1]

The first part of the liturgy of Good Friday, the service of the word, was to all intent and purposes the same as that of the Roman Missal of the time, except that the three deacons sang the Passion according to John barefoot and when they came to the words 'He gave up the spirit' *everyone* bent down and kissed the ground.

The veneration of the Cross had features of its own, in some ways closer to the *papal* liturgy of the day in the eighth century than that of the Roman Missal of 1570. For example the cross, veiled, *stands* before the people as in early Rome.

While the cross is brought in two priests in black copes sing the first of the Reproaches, *Popule meus* and two others sing the *Trisagion* in Greek, *Agios o Theos*, wearing red copes. To the *Agios* young clerics respond in Latin, *Sanctus Deus*, and so on throughout the Reproaches. Meanwhile the cross covered with a linen veil is standing before the people. The celebrant in alb and stole, and barefoot and with arms folded in the form of a cross makes three genuflections. The deacon and subdeacon do likewise. Then the celebrant uncovers the cross with a rod *(baguette)* and intones the *Ecce lignum crucia*. The ministers, servers and (presumably the people) venerate the cross while antiphons and other chants are sung. Two subdeacons sing the *Pange lingua gloriosi*, standing near the cross. The communion service that followed (called erroneously the 'Mass of the Presanctified') was more elaborate than the present rite but the people did not go to holy communion.

The Easter Vigil service (celebrated on Saturday morning!) was again much as it was in the Roman rite before 1955. The following differences may be noted. The service began with a litany while the new fire was being kindled and blessed. This is the first of the litanies sung during the course of the rite. After the ceremonies connected with the Paschal Candle there appear to be only four scripture readings, as in the time of St Gregory the Great. While they and the graduals are sung priests prepare catechumens for baptism. Whether this was an archaic touch of Le Tourneux's or whether there were in fact catechumens to be baptised it is difficult to say. In a Paris officially Catholic (apart from Huguenots) it is difficult to imagine that there were any adult catechumens to be instructed. It may be a reflection of the practice in Rome where a Jewish child was often baptised on Holy Saturday. During the procession to the font for the blessing of the water the second litany was sung though interrupted while the rites of the font took place. It was continued afterwards while the ministers disappeared into the sacristy to put on white vestments for the Mass.

At the Vespers of Easter Day an ancient custom was observed. Before the fourth psalm *(Laudate pueri)* there was a procession to the font, and the *In exitu* (the fifth psalm) was sung on the return journey during which various stations were made at different points in the church.

Altogether the Holy Week liturgy in Paris in the seventeenth century was a curious and interesting mixture of the old and the not so old, of the local and the Roman.

The third book of Le Tourneux that deserves comment is his

Priéres pour le Temps de l'avent appelées les O de Noël.[2] The 'O's of
Advent are the antiphons beginning with 'O' (e.g. *O Sapientia*)
that in the Roman rite are sung from December 17th to the 24th,
seven in number. In Paris there were nine and in some other places
eight. They are set to a noble and moving chant and in former
days were very popular – as they were, if we are to believe Le
Tourneux, in Paris. He speaks of great crowds of people going to
church 'to unite their prayers and voices' in singing the antiphons of the Church, the Bride of Christ, who is awaiting the
coming of her Bridegroom. Almost everyone, he continues, is
moved by a special devotion on these holy days when they see
the whole church united, the ministers of God in choir, religious
souls in their solitudes, lay people of every condition and sex[3] in
the churches. He speaks too of the one who presides intoning
each antiphon and who is the image of Jesus Christ, just as the
choir is the image of the body of which Christ is the Head. He is
envisaged as being present at the celebration. These remarks
show that Le Tourneux in his own way had a theology of the
active presence of Christ in the liturgy.

In the Roman rite the antiphons are sung twice, once before and
once after the Magnificat. In Paris they were sung three times,
though Le Tourneux does not tell us how they were arranged. It
was no doubt a Paris or French custom.

Along with his translations of the antiphons Le Tourneux includes translations of the collects of the four Sundays of Advent
and adds other prayers and '*Aspirations*' which are of a moralising kind. His comments on the antiphons themselves, so full of
Biblical and Christological meaning, are frankly disappointing.

The book by which Le Tourneux's name lived was his *L'Année
chrétienne* which appeared after his death, in the years 1682-
1701. The whole was complete by 1728. Like his translation of
the *Bréviaire* it became a storm centre, it was condemned by
bishops, put on the Roman Index of 1691 and thoroughly
disapproved of by all except those devout souls who took it to
church on Sunday mornings, as they did for many years to
come. The *gravamina* against Le Tourneux were that he had used
the translations of the scripture readings from Voison's already
condemned translations of the missal, that he had included a
translation of the Canon of the Mass and that his commentaries

included Jansenist or Jansenising teaching. Henri Bremond in his *Histoire du sentiment religieux en France* (t. XI, p 158-238) averred that he could not find the *'venin janséniste'* in the book. His commentaries are gloomy and present a rigorous kind of spirituality but that is not Jansenist. Le Tourneux was an ascetic and he seems to have wanted everyone to be one also. There is not much joy in his teaching but there is a deep and hidden glow which indicates a piety rarely openly expressed.

Why then was this many-volumed and on the whole gloomy book so popular? The first reason is that he provided an accurate translation of the Ordinary and Canon of the Mass, the texts of which came at the beginning of each volume. Secondly, there were the epistles and gospels of all the Sundays and feasts of the year, including those of the saints during the week. With these are to be included his commentaries on the scripture readings which are the heart of the work. Thirdly, each day is concluded with a prayer written by Le Tourneux. I suspect that he prayed always with a pen in his hand.

One feature of the *Année chrétienne* is that Le Tourneux's commentaries are all on the scripture texts of the missal. He offers no commentaries on the liturgical texts. It may be that he thought of himself as primarily a scripture exegete. He had written a *Life of Jesus Christ*, a commentary on the Epistle to the Romans and had translated some psalms. He had studied not only Greek, and of course Latin, but also Hebrew, knowledge he uses to make discreet corrections in his translation from the Vulgate. In an age when there was much 'figurative' and allegorical interpretation Le Tourneux stands out as one who seeks and expounds the literal meaning of the Bible texts. Like any Catholic of the time, however, especially one who had spent so much time studying the liturgy, he used typology where and when it was appropriate.

His *Année chrétienne* has often been contrasted with Guéranger's *Année Liturgique*. Whereas the latter introduced vast numbers of people to the liturgical texts and thus helped them to a better understanding of the whole of the liturgy, Le Tourneux concentrated on the biblical texts and by thus doing informed and enlightened his many readers – by no means all Jansenists – on the holy scriptures. In any case, there Sunday by Sunday and almost day by day they were confronted with the biblical texts which was important in an age that was anti-biblical. There is reason to believe also that he strengthened the prayer-life of those who used his book. The prayers with which he liked to conclude his considerations on the daily reading will have led people into prayer of their own. One example of the prayers he wrote, one that has great warmth, shows how he could lead people to pray on the Bible. It is based on the Hymn of Charity of 1 Corinthians 13:

> 'O charity, source of all that is good, without which nothing serves for our salvation, charity that is of absolute necessity, whose excellence is infinite, charity that lasts for ever; charity that is God himself, fire our hearts, come and take possession of us, and give yourself to us so that we may cease to belong to ourselves and belong entirely to him, apart from whom we are nothing and in whom we can find all our happiness and perfection' (*AC*, t. 2, p 229).

Bibliography

There is no biography of Nicholas Le Tourneux. A sympathetic short account (with bibliography) can be found in the *Dictionnaire de Spiritualité*, Fasc. LXI (1976), s.v. 'Le Tourneux'. Otherwise one can gather something of the man from the many books he wrote.

Notes

1. See Moléon, *Voyages liturgiques* (1718, Gregg, 1969), p 247.

2. It is not quite certain that this book is by Le Tourneux. Its author is unnamed but there are external signs as well as internal evidence that it is his.

3. '*de tout sexe*'!

CHAPTER VIII

England: Movement among the Recusant Catholics

Given the circumstances in which the English Catholics had to live from 1559 (the year of the Acts of Supremacy and Uniformity) it is not surprising that they could do nothing but to hand on to what was left to them. What was left was the memory of the restoration under Mary Tudor and for older people the rich, perhaps over rich, Catholic life into which they had been born and in which they grew up. There remained the Henrician and Marian priests most of whom conformed to the new situation but of these some continued to say Mass, the old Sarum rite of course, even if they read the services of the Book of Common Prayer in church. There were others who made the communion services of the Prayer Book look as much like the Mass as possible by muttering the words (probably inserting Latin words from the missal) and by turning their backs on the congregation.[1] Finally, there were those who refused to conform, who left their livings, went into hiding, saying Mass and shriving people who invited them, and yet others who went abroad to Louvain and France. When the seminary priests returned in the 1570s they used the revised Roman rite promulgated by Pius V in 1570. This was certainly a change though we have no information whether it was welcomed or not. The differences between the *said* Mass of the Sarum rite and the said Mass of the revised Roman rite were not very considerable. What was more important is that the seminary priests from the English College, Douai (and after 1579 from Rome) brought about a renewal of faith and practice. They said Mass where they were invited, they heard confessions (for which the laity had a great desire), they preached, usually after Mass. The laity had a great enthusiasm for sermons! In the minds of these recusant Catholics after 1575 there was always the thought of martyrdom, the first taking place in 1577 (St Cuthbert Mayne) and others coming with ever increasing numbers in the 1580s. There was no possibility of a liturgical movement;

all the recusants wanted was the Mass, the sacrament of Penance and prayer. As far as one can judge, partly from the literature of the time, the recusant community was a strongly praying community.

From the last decade of the sixteenth century a continual stream of Primers and Manuals of Prayer was published and went on being published until the nineteenth century. The Manuals of Prayer were not just prayer books of the sort people in the nineteenth century took to church. They were books that provided material for daily prayer and Christian living. There were prayers for morning and evening and others for 'noontide' but there was also a series of prayer-meditations on the Passion of Christ that indicates prayer was not to be just vocal. In addition to this these books usually included the little Offices of the Holy Cross and the Holy Ghost which, if shorn of psalms and readings, provided prayers for the various hours of the day. They were as it were parallel offices to that of the clergy. There were the Litanies, one of the Saints and the other the Golden Litany which recalled the main events of Christ's life from his birth to his passion, death and resurrection and had long been popular. With the latter we find 'prayers of Sir Thomas More while in prison'.

As has been the custom from the fourteenth and fifteenth centuries, there was what is best described as a prayer-commentary that followed the action of the Mass which of course was in Latin. These prayers are more or less paraphrases of the Latin texts though Gloria is given in English as is the Sanctus, both of which one must assume the worshippers recited silently. Since holy communion was rarely given during the Mass there were long prayers to be recited before and after it as well as prayers before and after confession.

The Manual I have examined is dated 1614 but its first edition, rather thinner, goes back to 1583 and its devotional stance is rather backward-looking. This is evident in the material provided for the Mass and also for the section called 'Manner to help a priest say Mass'. The server is called 'clarke' in medieval style, there are one or two reminiscences of the Sarum rite: the *Pax* or Peace is still given by what was called the *instrumentum pacis*, a metal plate of silver or brass with a design of the Lamb on it which the 'clarke' presented to the people to kiss; after communion the same man presented a chalice of wine to the communicants.

This was not a 'substitute' for the consecrated wine but for the cleansing of the mouth after receiving.

The provision made by the Manual of 1614 was generous. From the collection of prayers and other texts including psalm 94 (the *Venite*), the Lord's prayer in Latin (which in the Middle Ages all were expected to know) and the *Te Deum* in English we can see how people who could not get to Mass regularly (and there must have been many of them) could pray suitably at home on a Sunday morning.

One last item, showing considerable compassion for what was often a dangerous experience in the sixteenth and seventeenth centuries, namely child-birth, constitutes a little rite of its own. It begins with the *Sub tuum*, 'We fly to your protection, Holy Mother of God ...' and there follows a series of prayers, one to the Father, one to the Son, and one to the Holy Spirit (a common pattern at the time). There is a final prayer to St Mary which echoes the Hail Mary: the mother and those around her are directed to say 'A salutation to our Blessed Ladie' with a versicle and response 'Blessed the fruit of her womb and make haste to help her'.[2]

We are concerned with liturgical movement and active participation and its possible development in our period. The device used in the manuals was a continuation of the late medieval effort to attach people to the celebration of the Mass by means of a prayer-commentary that follows its action. The well known example is that of the *Layfolks Mass Book* which is of Norman-French origin and appeared in English in the thirteenth century. So early it seems was the difficulty for the people in taking part in a Latin Mass realised. In fact the device or similar ones went on being used right into the twentieth century until the Liturgical Movement began making an impact. There were others however in the oppressed church of the recusants who made a step forward. These priests were not content that people should be present, saying their own private prayers but they wanted them to take some part in the Mass and indeed other services. From the time of the Restoration of the monarchy in the seventeenth century there came a stream of popular books designed for that purpose.[3]

The first of these, called *The Great Sacrifice of the New Law ex-*

pounded by the figures of the Old ... was written by James Dymock, probably a scion of the ancient Catholic family of Lincolnshire. It first appeared in 1676 and by 1687 had run into eight editions. It was evidently popular. The first thing to be noted about it is that Dymock provides an English translation of whole of the Ordinary and of the Canon of the Mass (as well as the proper for Trinity Sunday and the Mass for the Dead). This may seem to be a fact of no importance but we need to remember that Pope Alexander VII, as recently as 1661, had explicitly forbidden and condemned translations of the missal into the vernacular, making special mention of the Canon. Dymock will have known about this, he graduated Doctor of Divinity from the Sorbonne in Paris and must have known the French scene well. Why then did he seem to disobey an important ruling such as that? The prohibition was foisted on the church through the machinations of Cardinal Mazarin for political purposes. His enemy was Paul de Gondi, Cardinal-Archbishop of Paris, whom Mazarin wanted to denigrate. Later, in France, the prohibition was ignored and so respectable a character as Bossuet said it had never been obeyed. Dymock may well have known about the dubious goings-on of Mazarin and did not feel bound by the prohibition. It is worth noting that it is probably the first English translation of the Canon ever to appear.

The second point to be noted is his theology of the laity. He sees them as sharing in the priesthood of Christ. There is first the priesthood of the ordained but there is a second which is 'common to all living members of the Church so that by the title of Christian we share in the Priesthood of Christ, of which we are made partakers in our baptism by the Unction of Chrisma, on the child's head'. This was the basis of Dymock's theology of active participation: all 'joyntly offer it (the Mass) with the priest: this sacrifice being ours no less than his. It is our Host or Victim, it is our Oblation, which he offers with us, and we with him, and which he and we together with the Triumphant Church, offer to God the Father by his Son' (p 9). He repeats this later: 'the people are to joyn as much as they can both with the Actions and Prayers of the Priest' and he takes occasion to have a stab at those who do not attempt to act as he would have them: he rebukes 'those who go to see and be seen ... in pompous apparel, full of Pride and Vanity, "Going stately into the House of Israel".' He was writing in the more relaxed days of the Restoration and may have had his eye on the court Catholics who attended the Queen's chapel in Whitehall.

That he did not leave his teaching up in the air and that he expected some vocal participation can be gathered from directives or suggestions that he gives at certain points. After the sign of the cross the Mass began with a psalm (42) and after it in his text he adds 'The People Answer'. The same directive appears after the *Orate, fratres* (Pray, brethren ...). He knew of the offertory procession as it still existed in the Ambrosian Rite (with which he was familiar) and also on certain feasts in churches of France. At the Memento for the Living in the Canon he recommends that the names of those to be prayed for should be read out 'as is still done in the Gallican church' on the four solemnities of Christmas, Easter, Whitsunday and All Saints. He assumes people will receive communion at the right time, after the priest's communion. The rite of the Latin Mass as envisaged by Dymock was a very satisfactory one and could be said to have been an anticipation of the Dialogue Mass that came into use from at least the 1930s until Vatican II when the liturgy was translated into vernaculars.[4]

John Goter or Gother, a younger contemporary of James Dymock, was one of the most important influences on the Catholic Community in the eighteenth century and even beyond. He was, it seems, of French Huguenot stock who in his early youth was a Presbyterian and equally early became a Catholic. He went to the English College, Lisbon, for studies and arrived back in England the year before Charles II died (1682). He was appointed as the chief controversialist to the community and his work was regarded as important. During the reign of James II he was one of the staff of the Catholic chapel opened at the Fishmongers Hall where Dymock was a colleague. After the Glorious Revolution Dymock retired to France and Goter was to be found by 1689 at Warkworth Castle near Banbury, the home of George Holman who had married the Lady Anastasia, daughter of the martyred Viscount Stafford (1680).

He was a prolific writer and his style is said to have been admired by John Dryden but much was what we would call moralistic. He had very strict notions about keeping the Sunday (and the greater feast-days) holy. At the same time he had a considerable compassion for the lot of working-class people whether as servants in the great houses (even the Catholic ones) or in other lowly jobs where they were without protection of any kind. Always in his writing there is a sense of the vulnerability of such people.[5] He was also much occupied in writing on what we should call liturgy. Here we consider only two of his books. From these we can gather that, like Dymock and other recusant priests, he was not satisfied with the current ways of 'hearing Mass'. He wanted people to understand the rite and to take part in it in whatever way was possible at the time.

The first of his books I mention here was evidently directed to understanding. Before his sudden and much lamented death at sea on his way to Lisbon to become rector there he had been preparing the book that was called *The Holy Mass in Latin and English* (in later editions as *The Roman Missal in Latin and English*) which appeared in 1718. Goter's papers had been put together and edited by a William Crathorne with the approval of the Vicar Apostolic of the London District. This last point is important as Goter had translated the whole of the missal including the Canon of the Mass. It is highly improbable that he did not know of the prohibition of Pope Alexander VII and perhaps he thought it did not apply in England. In any case he saw a pastoral need and decided to meet it.

Goter's translation of the Roman Missal had a twofold importance. Apart from Voisin's condemned French translation, Goter's (and possibly Pellison's) is the first vernacular translation ever to appear in Europe. As has been said above, various attempts had been made to secure the publication of translations of the Ordinary of the Mass but nothing more. For whatever reason Goter's translation was never condemned and it could be said that he set a certain pattern. He had followers of one kind or another, the chief of whom was Dr Husenbeth who in 1837 brought out his complete translation of the missal which seems to owe something to Goter's. The second reason for its importance is that it went on being published until the end of the eighteenth century and it must therefore have been used.

It is possible however that a more modest book was even more important. *The Roman Missal* was in three volumes and the cost must have put it out of the range of the poor. Long before the publication of the missal there appeared *Instructions and Devotions for hearing Mass; for Confession, Communion and Confirmation*.[6] It could be said to be a liturgical manual for the ordinary Catholic.

It begins with a Catechism in which Goter sets out the theological basis for the people's participation in the Mass which in doctrine and sometimes almost verbally is the same as Dymock's. He also shows from the structure and texts of the Mass, e.g. the prayers are in the plural, that it is the action of a community and not simply of one man, the priest. He sums up his teaching: 'as many of the faithful, as desire to conform to the spirit of the Church ... ought to go to Mass with the intention of offering to Almighty God, with the priest, the great sacrifice of the body and blood of Christ, and consequently be very careful to accompany him, if not in all, at least in the principal parts; that so, by this means, they may more effectually partake of the fruits of it' (p 8). At the same time he is easy about those who can do no more than say the rosary. More explicitly and echoing both Le Tourneux and Dymock he lays down the basis of what we should call active participation: 'It is the priest alone that consecrates, but it is not to be imagined, it is he alone that is to offer the victim, no, the Mass is the sacrifice of the whole Church, that is, both of priest and people; therefore, as the priest offers it to Almighty God, so ought likewise people offer it, both with the priest and by him' (p 4).

Goter continues his 'catechism' with a statement of the four ends of the Mass, the first of which is to honour God (duty, obligation), the second is thanksgiving (only loosely connected with remembrance), the third is propitiatory (the application to us of the merits of Christ's passion) and the fourth is petition when with the Church we ask for God's blessings both spiritual and temporal. It is in this context that Goter rebukes the lazy whose 'posture of kneeling on one knee seems to be paying duty to a demi-god'. Others stare about, yet others are 'profanely whispering or conversing' and there are those who appear 'in their vanities'; overdressed ladies we may suspect. Goter demanded reverence, a reverence he himself shows in his writing.

Goter lays out four methods of 'hearing Mass' of which only the first two need concern us here. The third is the conventional one for the devout (the 'Advanced') that is, pious sentiments to fit various parts of the Mass, and the fourth is for the 'Absent' which consists of one psalm (83) and prayers following the action of the Mass.

The First Method, intended for 'Young Beginners' who may be children preparing to make their First Communion (about the age of twelve, as was the custom) or, we may suspect not very literate converts who are new to the church or just approaching it. Goter recommends that they should go to Mass for eight or ten *days* though one wonders whether he means successively. They are to spend their time simply looking though it is expected that there will be a 'christian friend' with the neophyte to name and point out the different parts of the Mass. Even so, some prayers are provided that follow its action. What however is unusual is that Goter attaches to his Method twenty-six short texts and responses in Latin and English taken from the rite of the Mass. These range from the *Dominus vobiscum* with its response to whole texts such as the *Gloria*, the *Credo*, the *Sanctus*, the *Pater noster* and the *Agnus Dei*. The inclusion of these texts in English and Latin (Goter expected the priest to say Mass in a way that could be heard by all) was meant to be both a guide to the one 'hearing the Mass' and a means of learning some simple Latin. Goter was always the catechist, always the teacher.

One feels that his 'Second Method for the Well Instructed' was the one most favoured by him (pp 32–93). Here was the whole Ordinary of the Mass with the Canon translated into English which with some tinkering by Crathorne, appears in his Roman Missal. It is all clearly set out, one part separated from another with summaries of the rubrics in between. Here is Goter's method in full: following the action of the Mass as it was said and praying it as well as possible, i.e. using the translated texts, though Goter, on the pages opposite to the liturgical texts places prayers, all rather individualistic in style. It is difficult to know why he did this; one must suppose that in this at least he was conforming to what had become a custom.

The question arises whether Goter expected the people to reply vocally. As first sight it looks as if he did. All the dialogue parts of the Mass (e.g. the dialogue before the Preface) have the letters P. and A. standing for 'Priest' and 'Answer'. At the beginning of the Mass there is this directive: 'The people may answer the priest as is set down in the other (?) page or say as follows, 'In the name of the Father ...'. It is not clear what 'the other page' refers to. It seems to refer to the *opposite* page where the liturgical texts are given, though of course in English. Doubt is dispelled however by other directives as on page 36 where we read that the Clerk (i.e. the server) says the *Confiteor* in the name of the people. When we read (p 47) that the people may say the Creed with the priest it is clear that they are to say it in English, no doubt silently, while the priest says it in Latin. That anyone should have prayed this and other texts *aloud* is unlikely - after the departure of James II there were no public churches and Masses were private – but like Dymock Goter may have been aware of the practice of vocal participation as practised in certain Jansenist churches in France. I think it is fair to say that he would have *liked* the people to answer and pray with the priest.

If it be thought that even Goter's Instructions would have been too much for the barely literate and the poor there is evidence that small cheap booklets giving the substance of the Ordinary of the Mass were in circulation at a cost of a few pence each.[7] The level of literacy was rising in the eighteenth century and what Challoner called 'the middling class' of artisans, craftsmen, small business men and the rest was steadily expanding. The clergy were very busy instructing and through them the new kind of Catholic will have been initiated into an understanding of the Mass and other rites of the Church. In the early years of the nineteenth century (from 1809 to 1832) small, even pocket, editions of the missal in translation appeared, one of which in the possession of a school boy was very well thumbed. Finally Dr Husenbeth's *The Missal for the use of the Laity* ... appeared in 1837 and went on being published to the end of the century. The English Catholics were better provided with liturgical books to suit their needs than any other country in Europe or, unless these English missals were exported, than in the United States of America.

Richard Challoner would be said to have dominated the second half of the eighteenth century except that he was a self-effacing man who 'dominated' by what he provided for the people not only of his own age but of the nineteenth century as well. Educated at English College, Douai, he graduated D.D. at the university there and taught theology at the college. He was eventually called to England and in 1741 was made Co-adjutor bishop to Dr Petre, Vicar Apostolic of the London District, whom he succeeded in 1758. He was above all the great catechist though his notion of catechesis was very broad. It embraced the whole range of Christian teaching, from the Bible of which he produced a revised and more modern edition, to history, the lives of the saints, a simple catechism for young children, material for the spiritual life (he translated afresh the *Imitation of Christ* and St Francis de Sales' *Introduction to the Devout Life*) and much else too. He concerned himself with the liturgy, editing an *Ordo administrandi Sacramenta* (for the use of the clergy) with specimen homilies to be used when administering the sacraments.

The book however by which he was known for some 200 years was the *Garden of the Soul* that appeared in 1740. It has usually been thought of as merely a prayer book of the sort that people took to church. It was much more than that. Working within the tradition of the old Manual he provided for the Christian life of ordinary Christians. There is some simple instruction on the faith, there is much prayer content, for night and morning for instance, helps for meditation and prayers before and after communion. He was a disciple of Goter but his method of hearing Mass was more cautious than his. He does not give a translation of the Canon though he showed considerable skill in paraphrasing that text and other texts of the Ordinary of the Mass. In another book *The Catholic Christian instructed in the Sacraments, Sacrifice ... of the Church* (1737) he expresses his reservations about people reading the Canon though in the same book he refers his readers to Goter's *Instruction and Devotions for Hearing Mass*. Also included in the book were Vespers and Compline for Sundays.

It is a book that endured and its sober piety gave the name to those Catholics who were known as 'Garden of the Soul Catholics'. Challoner himself added to the book in his own lifetime, others did likewise in the nineteenth century though as the years went by much was removed and newer devotions ousted the old. By the twentieth century it was hardly recognisable. This was a pity. It was a book that had kept alive for great numbers of Catholics some minimal notion of the liturgy and the need for prayer in daily life.

About the time of the Catholic Relief Acts (1778, 1791) there is observable a change of mood that partly reflected a change in the composition of the Catholic community. Small churches began to be built in towns and cities, the clergy were becoming more like parish priests instead of 'missionary priests' or chaplains to the nobility and gentry. They had greater freedom of action and used it to gather their flocks and to instruct them. But it was mostly among the laity that the change in mood came. They were showing signs of independence; it was they who negotiated the First Relief Act (1778) without consultation with the Vicars Apostolic and were largely responsible for the Second Relief Act. They wanted proper diocesan bishops who would be less dependent on Rome for their powers (faculties) but would have them by Canon Law. Some of them seem to have been influenced by what has been called '*The English Catholic Enlightenment*'.[8]

No doubt it was mostly among some of the nobility and gentry that 'enlightened' or 'liberal' view were held. Perhaps they derived them from the continent where the '*époque des lumiéres*' in France and the *Aufklärung* in the Germanies had long been the dominant philosophy. As we have already seen, the emphasis was on instruction and the liturgy itself was regarded as something that should teach. In the English situation the clergy wanted the people to understand the liturgy and to follow it as closely as possible. This was to go no further than Dymock or Goter but in the new atmosphere some of the clergy and some of the laity said that understanding could be delivered by the liturgy itself if it were in the language of the people. Explicit examples of this mentality are the following.

Sir John Throckmorton who in the eighteenth century lived mostly at Weston Underwood in Bedfordshire, had as a near neighbour the poet William Cowper who was a low church Protestant. From time to time he used to invite him to dinner when he met Throckmorton's chaplain, William Gregson, a Benedictine whom Cowper found, as he said, an agreeable and reasonable man. One night Cowper remarked that all professions affect an air of mystery like doctors who prescribe in Latin to the peril of their patients' lives. Throckmorton, turning to his chaplain said, 'That is just as absurd as our praying in Latin'. Gregson evidently agreed for he published a book on the lines of the Book of Common Prayer. The bishop of the London District condemned it.

In the same context we find pleas for some English in the liturgy. Joseph Berington, a learned and somewhat provocative writer, and well acquainted with Throckmorton and his circle, wrote a pamphlet with the apparently innocuous title *A Letter on the use of the Latin tongue in the service*. In this he proposed 'that the part of the Altar Service which is read aloud should be read in English' if the authorities of the Church should permit. The authorities of the Church of course did not permit but the Letter brought an interesting response from John Carroll, the first Archbishop of Baltimore in the United States, who wrote urging Berington to publish something more 'on the use of the vernacular in worship'. Whether as a consequence or not, in another pamphlet later he included a condemnation of Latin in worship. He was something of an *enfant terrible* and was particularly disliked by Bishop Milner, Vicar Apostolic of the Midland District.

The pastoral clergy however were concerned that when the people came to church that they should pray. Evidence of this are the several editions of the Manual of Prayer (rather different from the seventeenth century ones) where a series of vernacular prayers is provided to be read out by the priest before the principal Mass on Sundays. An elaborate example of this sort of thing is found in a surprising quarter. Its title indicates its content: *Prayers to be said before and after Mass and in the Afternoon on all Sundays and Festivals in the Catholic Chapel of Worcester*. This was a Jesuit church. The book was published in Worcester in 1822 and from an examination of its contents it was evidently not the first edition. What is surprising is that before Mass there is a whole office (which must have taken nearly half-an-hour) which contained the *Venite* (ps 94/95) two psalms, a hymn 'To God from whom all blessings flow' by John Wesley, the *Benedictus* and other prayers. It was based on the office of Lauds but with a distinctly Anglican flavour. The Afternoon Service was pretty well Vespers but with the 'Prayer of St John Chrysostom' as found in the Book of Common Prayer! All of course was in English.

Here was an 'assimilation' to Anglican worship, a word used by the learned and sober historian by Dr John Lingard who was in favour of drawing Anglicans closer to the Catholic Church. He was also in favour of the people taking some part (only a small part) in the celebration of Mass. In his own new and revised

Manual of Prayer the 'I confess' was given in English and he allowed the people to say it and the absolution that followed. He
was in favour of the whole of the Burial Service being done in
English, and on Palm Sunday he appointed a layman to read the
Passion in English while he said it in Latin at the altar. This practice
proved so popular that people came from Lancaster, ten miles
away, to attend this service. He did not think too much of the
Douai-Challoner translation of the Bible and so he himself made
a translation of the four gospels. He was a good Greek scholar.
One reason why Lingard wanted change in the liturgy was ecumenical. He wanted worship, liturgical and other, to be sufficiently attractive to draw Anglicans to think better of the
Catholic Church. He made a plea for 'ecclesiastical reconciliation'
and asked that on his tomb should be the words, 'Here lies an
advocate for the union of Christians'.[9]

Whatever may be thought of the details, it is to the credit of the
recusancy clergy and their immediate followers that in one way
or another they realised that liturgy is for the people and belongs to the people. To borrow the words of Pius XI (and the
Constitution on the Liturgy), they did not want them to be merely
silent spectators and they did what they could within the con-
ventions of their time to attach the people to the action of the
Mass. In however limited a way they can be said to have promoted a pastoral liturgy.

In spite of efforts to bring about some change the condition of
worship remained much the same in most places. Details of the
worship in a school chapel on Sundays about the end of the
eighteenth century (and no doubt rather earlier also) can be
found in a *History of Sedgley Park and Cotton College* (by Frank
Roberts, Preston, 1985, pp 41–2): 'After prayers, the chaplain
would read the Epistle and Gospel of the day, and preach, or
read a sermon. A Low Mass followed, after which Prayers after
Mass were read …'. The Procurator's books of the day show that
many of the boys bought their own missals. Others used the
'Garden of the Soul' or some other prayer book. Vespers were
said in the afternoon, 'the boys reciting the alternate verses of the
psalms'. It must have been rather dull. Benediction was given
only rarely and then with scant ceremony. One boy served in his
ordinary clothes and the thurible was brought in from the
kitchen at the appropriate time. Some singing was introduced in
later years.

Notes

1. See Christopher Haigh, *English Reformations* (1993) p 253.

2. See my *Worship in a Hidden Church*, Columba Press, Dublin, 1988, pp 34–43.

3. See my *Worship in a Hidden Church*, pp 55–74.

4. For a fuller account see *Worship in a Hidden Church*, pp 55–58.

5. See his *Instructions for Particular States and Conditions of Life*, ch. XIII, 'for laborious or working Christians' (vol IX).

6. *The Spiritual Works of Rev John Goter*. In Sixteen Volumes, Vol X, Newcastle (upon Tyne), 1792?

7. See *Worship in a Hidden Church*, p 79.

8. See *The English Catholic Enlightenment* 1780–1850 by Joseph P. Chinnici, Patmos Press, Sheperdstown, USA, 1980.

9. For the foregoing see *Worship in a Hidden Church*, pp 92–103.

CHAPTER IX

The Gothic Revival

By the 1830s Catholics were beginning to look old-fashioned. They were a quiet people and did not want to draw attention to themselves. Apart from a few churches in London and perhaps elsewhere the liturgy was of the low variety. Where the mass was sung the music was of the sort deeply affected by secular music. In London opera singers, usually Catholics from Italy, went to church on Sundays and sang perhaps with the choir but certainly solo; even the Credo was sung in that way by a famous soprano. The church buildings were undistinguished, trailing feeble clouds of rococo glory. A change was necessary but what was it to be? The Romantics, Coleridge, Wordsworth, Walter Scott, had turned people's minds to the long-despised Middle Ages and this began to affect church people not only in England but on the continent. Into this scene stepped the young Augustus Welby Pugin (1812–1852), a man of vast energy and a brilliant imagination. He dreamed of covering once again the whole of the country with Gothic spires and pointed windows (see his *Contrasts*) but his dreams rarely came true. His best church is almost certainly St Giles, Cheadle, North Staffordshire, where he had a free hand as the Earl of Shrewsbury was paying the bills. What however is important from our viewpoint here is that he was a liturgist or, in the nineteenth century vocabulary, a liturgiologist. His churches were meant to be expressions of a restored, that is, a medieval, liturgy and they were designed for its celebration. Moreover, he wanted to restore, as far as possible, the *way* that liturgy had been celebrated. He did not want tabernacles for the Reserved Sacrament on the high altar where they had not been in the Middle Ages. He therefore designed Blessed Sacrament chapels (see St Giles). For him the sanctuary of choir was a sacred place to which the *hoi polloi* might not be admitted. The story is well known of the shock of horror he felt when he saw Bishop Wiseman conducting *women* through the sanctuary of St Barnabas, Nottingham. He sat on a bench and wept. No, surpliced (not cotta-ed) choirs of men and boys must occupy the sanctuary (as from the beginning, 1841, at St Chad's Cathedral, Birmingham). Plainsong must be re-introduced and was. The old rites of medieval England must be restored, so he built Easter Sepulchres though it is doubtful that the clergy ever used them as he intended. Whatever is to be said about his idealism he certainly raised the standard of Catholic worship.

What however drove him on was not simply romanticism but a deep Christian spirit and an almost overwhelming desire to clear out of Catholic worship all the fripperies and levities that had crept into it. He travelled much on the continent studying the ancient Gothic churches and observing the worship that took place inside them. He expected to find the medieval style of worship that had, he supposed, continued uninterrupted through the centuries. He was to be bitterly disappointed. In Cologne he entered the great Gothic Domkirche with awe, imagining that he would be attending a service in keeping with the majesty of the building. There were great crowds of people jostling one another and then 'a wretched handful of canons' pushed their way through them to their stalls which were otherwise occupied by laypeople, many of whom Pugin judged were Protestants. The Mass began with a prelude of violins, the choirmaster then came in accompanied by some fashionably dressed women, holding their music. There then followed an enormous burst of music from the orchestra which he concluded was meant to stand for the Kyrie. He does not describe the rest of the liturgy but ends by saying that he felt he was not longer in a cathedral but at some sort of concert in a Winter Garden.[1] His final comment was that this was the sort of thing that happened when 'the ancient choral chant was given up'.

Pugin's liturgical movement could be said to be a movement in reverse. He was thinking of the liturgy as it was in the Middle Ages; if he was not explicit about it, he would have been glad to restore the rite of Sarum. But three centuries had passed, the Roman rite had been tidied up (1568, 1570) and made more rigid with its system of rubrics. Many medieval customs had died out, like the giving of the *Pax* with the Pax-Brede or *Instrumentum pacis* and the placing of the consecrated host in the 'sepulchre' to be 'raised again' on the morning of Easter Day. Pugin liked the 'dim religious light', most of his churches are (or were) dark, every window if possible filled with stained glass. The Rood and the screen dividing the people from the clergy was of the essence of his liturgical views and if you wanted to remain a friend of Pugin you had to be a 'Rood and Screen' man – Nicholas Wiseman, though kind to him, was not, nor was John Henry Newman. Other Tractarians who remained in the Church of England cultivated the Gothic and their architects like Butterfield and Bodley produced some good churches. Indeed it could be said that the Anglicans inherited Pugin's legacy. It was they who in parish churches set up the surpliced choirs, it was they who insisted on a devout liturgy and throughout the nineteenth century fostered good liturgical music. If there was liturgical movement in England it was in the Church of England and it was Anglican scholars who studied and published ancient liturgical documents – to the envy of continental scholars.

Whether Nicholas Wiseman should be included in this panorama of liturgical movers may be questioned. He certainly had a great love of the liturgy especially of the Roman/Papal sort. In his *Lectures on Holy Week* (1838) delivered in Rome the year before to a miscellaneous audience which seems to have included non-catholics he shows a very considerable knowledge of the history of the liturgy both East and West and used Mabillon, de Vert and others in his description of the Holy Week liturgy as celebrated by the pope at the time. In his first lecture he had much to say about Christian art and architecture and reveals an admiration for the medieval Gothic which 'threw up all its lines, so as to bear the eye towards heaven' (p 19). There is a touch of the Romantic here. In his descriptions of the various rites he insists that they need to be understood. They are not mere show. They are signs expressing the meaning of the great events they recall. They represent, (though it is not quite clear what he means by that verb), 'they act rather than (merely) commemorate' and they as it were make present (though he does not use that word) what has happened in the past (p 39). He was concerned that the people he was talking to should go to the liturgy of Holy Week not as mere spectators but as people who would be willing to be affected in their minds and hearts by the rites, the music and, yes, the words of which the liturgy is made up. His commentaries on the music to be sung are notably well informed and discerning and must have been helpful to his audience and he has

some not unamusing observations to make on church music before the Council of Trent. He quotes a writer of 1549: 'They (the
singers) find their greatest happiness in contriving that while
one says (sings?) *sanctus*, the other should sing *Sabaoth*, and a
third *gloria tua*, with certain howlings, bellowings and gargling
noises so that they resemble rather cats in January than flowers
in May' (p 44 fn 1, slightly changed).

This is not the place to give a full account of the papal liturgy of
Holy Week but Wiseman preserves for posterity certain customs
that are now obsolete. He records that the Passions on Palm
Sunday and Good Friday were sung by choir-men (with gratifying
results) and not by clergymen. On Maundy Thursday the pope
washed the feet of thirteen 'poor priests' and gave them money
afterwards. One wonders how they were chosen. He is aware
that *Tenebrae* ought to be sung during the night but tells us that
in Rome it was sung at 4.00 p.m. on all three evenings,
Wednesday, Thursday and Friday. It was attended, at least on
the first two nights, by a numerous crowd (mostly tourists one
suspects) especially to hear the wonderful Allegri *Miserere* of
which Wiseman gives a very perceptive analysis.[2]

If people remember Wiseman at all they probably think of him
as celebrating grand ceremonies, which any way cannot have
been so grand, in St Mary's, Moorfields, which had to be turned
into something resembling a pro-cathedral. But he had a concern
for the people, he thought that they ought to know and understand the liturgy. To the long morning and evening prayers then
used (or were supposed to be used) Wiseman preferred Prime
and Compline, the prayers of the Church for those times. He
wanted the people to enter into the spirit of the liturgy and
thought that the missal, the ritual (i.e. the *Rituale*) and even the
Pontificale, in good translations, should be in the hands of the
laity.[3] Perhaps he did not know of Goter's work nor yet the existence of cheap and complete missals in circulation and use in the
first three decades of the century. Husenbeth's Missal came out
in 1837, the year the Lectures were given in Rome.

This aspect of Wiseman's liturgical outlook, largely unknown,
was in sharp contrast to the thinking and practice of some who
were propagating devotions of an Italian kind that, they
thought, would thus please him. Faber, it is true, can be said to

have given the Catholic Church in England its hymnal but his compositions have, it seems, died the death. Newman, who felt more comfortable with the old Catholics, wrote few hymns but they have endured, *Praise to the Holiest* and *Firmly I believe and truly*, both from his *Dream of Gerontius*. In the second half of the nineteenth century in England public worship largely consisted of the Mass, celebrated ever more correctly according to the rubrics of the *Missale Romanum*, and 'devotions' of various sorts and quality. There even seem to have been a diminution of liturgical knowledge among the laity at this time for Abbot Fernand Cabrol, reflecting on his experience of the early decades of the twentieth century, could write: 'The average English Catholic is not interested in the liturgy and does not even know what the word means. And if I ask a Catholic what Sunday it is or what is the liturgical season generally speaking he does not know'.[4] He was writing in the *Questions Liturgiqes et Paroissiales* in 1930, the year after the foundation of the Society of St Gregory which over the next thirty years propagated information about the liturgy and promoted active participation. It is of course still at work.

Notes

1. See O. Rousseau, *Histoire du Mouvement Liturgique*, Paris, 1945, p 118.

2. The lectures were published by the Catholic publisher Dolman in 1854: *Four Lectures on the Offices and Ceremonies of Holy Week, as performed in the Papal Chapels*. Delivered in Rome in the Lent of MDCCCXXXVII. By Nicholas Wiseman, D.D.

3. See O. Rousseau, op cit, pp 128–9.

4. cf Rousseau, op cit, p 127.

CHAPTER X

Daniel Rock

Liturgiologist

One of the long line of priests who did much to instruct the people in the liturgy was the now half-forgotten Daniel Rock who was, in England at least, probably the most learned liturgiologist of his time. His knowledge of liturgy, especially of the later medieval liturgy, was very extensive though perhaps not deep. He discovered no new MSS (though he worked from the MS of the Sarum Rite kept at Salisbury) and showed no evidence of scholarly insight of the kind that produces new theories or new points of view. He knew what had been done in the Middle Ages and he came to understand it very well to such a point that to read his *Church of our Fathers* is to understand something at least of medieval piety. Through his long scrutiny of medieval documents, books, stained-glass, sculpture, chalices, vestments and a dozen other things whose use and purpose we have forgotten he could reconstruct medieval worship, especially as it was celebrated in England. His was a considerable achievement especially when one remembers that his first book *Hierurgia* (on the Mass) was published when he was but thirty-four, when the Neo-Gothic movement was still in its infancy. That curious hybrid, Strawberry-Hill-Regency-Gothic, was of course well known but it was not until Augustus Welby Pugin began to insist on *The True Principles of Pointed or Christian Architecture* that people began to realise how a Gothic church was constructed and what it was for. Rock may not have known much about building but he certainly knew what Gothic churches were for. He almost certainly knew more about medieval liturgy, down to its smallest details, than any other man of his time, including Pugin. One piece of research that might be undertaken is to discover what influence, if any, Daniel Rock had on Pugin who did not become a Catholic until 1835. He was also in the field before the Cambridge Camden Society which was founded by J. M. Neale and B. Webb in 1839 and whose magazine *The Ecclesiologist* began to appear in 1841.

Whence did Daniel Rock acquire his interest in liturgical matters? For Catholics the time was not propitious. They were just emerging from the Penal Days and when Rock was a boy the Catholic Emancipation Bill had not been passed. Catholics were poor and not numerous and had to be content with cheap and hastily run up 'chapels' which harked back to the eighteenth century rather than to the Middle Ages though some of them had pointed windows. Otherwise they were just large rooms with an altar one end and pews filling the nave. Pugin was scornful of these edifices (ball rooms, he called them) though by the time he came to design and build churches, Catholics were becoming more venturous. However poorly they paid him they were his chief clients. But Rock's boyhood and youth had passed long before this state of affairs came to be.

He was born in 1799 in Liverpool into a family that had long been Catholics and he received his first education from the priest (a Benedictine) at St Peter's, Seel St. No doubt he was one of those learned priests of the age who knew their Greek and Latin classics very well and we may assume that he laid the foundations of the young Daniel's competence in these languages. In his writings he not only cites long passages from Latin authors of almost every age but he assumes his readers will have as much knowledge as himself of Greek. When he was about fourteen he went to St Edmund's College, Ware, which had undergone considerable expansion as it had taken in many of the 'refugees' from the English College, Douai. It was there that he was first initiated into what his biographer calls 'ecclesiastical architecture' by a priest called Louis Havard who had also come from Douai. In 1818 Rock went out to the English College, Rome, along with Nicholas Wiseman. The college had suffered less than was feared from the French occupying power and had but recently been opened, thanks to Cardinal Consalvi. Here Rock spent seven years until his graduation as Doctor of Divinity in 1825. Here too he made the acquaintance of the Honourable John Talbot who was shortly to become the sixteenth Earl of Shrewsbury. After Rock had spent two years in pastoral work in the old parish of St Mary, Moorfields, the Earl invited him to be his chaplain at Alton. We may suppose that Rock gladly assented as parish work was never his forte.

Rock's interest in the liturgy and the Christian past had been stimulated in Rome and he began to collect materials for a history of the Mass. To facilitate his research the Earl sent him back to Rome 'to study in libraries and the *catacombs*'! Rock of course knew his way around Rome and managed to get drawings made of those things he wished to remember and describe. These drawings were to stand him in good stead for some time to come. On his return to England he set to work and in 1833 produced his first book, *Hierurgia* which was apparently well received.

In spite of being much concerned with Pugin in the building of his Gothic extravaganza know as Alton Towers and of the new 'Christian' churches, the Earl spent a good deal of time abroad. Rock may not have cared to stay on at Alton while the master was away and so he moved to Buckland in Berkshire to become chaplain to Sir Robert Throckmorton. There Rock continued his studies but also looked after the people who lived in the area. He was gentle and kind and left a good memory among them.

By 1852 when he was made a Canon of the newly constituted diocese of Southwark, Rock was living in Kensington, without, it seems, any pastoral charge, and there he spent the rest of his days. Here 'his kindly disposition and widely-known scholarship made him a favourite with the more serious members of the literary and fashionable world'. His 'At Homes' on Thursday afternoons were attended by numbers of the nobility and learned classes', among them being Lord Houghton, Lord Romilly, Master of the Rolls, and Lord and Lady Holland. A rather Whig society.

There is some piquancy in the fact that this Romish priest should be holding a *salon* in the midst of the grim moralism of Victorian London. It harked back to eighteenth century France rather than to anything that was happening in the England of the time.

Rock's reputation as a medievalist and a liturgiologist was greatly enhanced by the appearance of his four volume *The Church of our Fathers* (1849–1853) which in spite of its often polemical tone was apparently well received. This and his *salon* led to his election to the Committee of the South Kensington Museum (later to be called the Victoria and Albert Museum) to which Rock made valuable contributions. Among gifts in kind were a portable altar which had belonged to Cardinal Bessarion and a copper-gilt thurible said to have belonged to Pope Boniface VIII. He contributed to the catalogue of an exhibition of Church vestments and later worked up his notes for what was to prove his last book *Textile Fabrics* which appeared one year before his death in 1871.[1]

The question that confronts us is what influence Rock had in his own time on the Gothic Revival and indeed whether he fits into the liturgical tradition of the English Catholic community. The first question is difficult to answer. We should need to know how widely his books were read and the number of copies that were printed. Both the *Hierurgia* and *The Church of Our Fathers* are (or were) to be found in the libraries of Catholic colleges and other institutions and presumably at one time they were read. Then there is the fact of the 1903 edition under Anglican auspices which would seem to indicate that Rock had had an influence in that Anglo-Catholic world that looked back to the Middle Ages rather than to the liturgy of the post-Tridentine church. Certainly the Anglican editors are generous in their praise of Rock's scholarship and, as they say in the Postscript (Volume IV), the fact that their list of corrections and subsequent liturgical studies is so short is a witness to the quality of his work. From another point of view Rock can be seen to be in the main stream of that liturgical movement of which Augustus Welby Pugin is the best known representative which sought to restore medieval worship in all its late exuberance.

Also from another point of view Rock can be seen to be in the main stream of Romanticism which looked with nostalgia on the medieval past which many Christians, both Catholics and Anglicans, wished to transform into a restoration of medieval liturgical and devotional practices. Like Augustus Welby Pugin, though less violently, Rock was in conscious reaction to the rococo forms of liturgy of the eighteenth century. Churches furnished with roods and screens with burning lights before altars and shrines, chantry chapels and the whole disorderly profusion of late medieval objects were what Rock and others wished to see restored to churches which Mr Pugin made unmistakably Gothic. In this both he and Rock were in accord with the liturgical restoration of the past that was being so ardently pursued by Abbot Guéranger in France and others less well known in Germany. As is well known, Pugin and others transformed the face of English Catholicism (not to mention Anglicanism) with his churches and with the now hieratic worship that went on in the buildings he put up. Not all was well of course and he complained that priests did not know how to use his churches and Rock gently laments that debased 'Roman' vestments were still being used that were wholly unsuited to the places where they were worn.

How far Rock saw that the people should have some active part in worship is not at all clear. Like his Penal Days predecessors and his contemporary F.C. Husenbeth he would have liked the people to *understand* the liturgy and to respond to its mysterious beauty. But in his writings there is no indication that he ever thought of them singing the liturgy or responding to it vocally.[2] His pastoral interest was in any case feeble and his pastoral experience very small. He was primarily a historian, a collector, a connoisseur, interested in objects for their own sake and as manifestations of a past that he must have realised could never return.

Notes

1. These details of Rock's life are gleaned from the memoir by Fr Bernard Kelly to be found in the Hart and Frere edition of *The Church of Our Fathers*, vol 1, pp xvii–xxvi (1903) whence also the quotations made above come.
2. In his *Church of Our Fathers* Rock rather pathetically expresses his desire for the restoration of the Bidding Prayers as known in the Middle Ages.

CHAPTER XI

Two Anglican Liturgists

The Church of England has had a long and distinguished line of liturgical scholars from the beginning of the nineteenth century (to go no further back) until now. They have studied texts ancient and modern, they have edited many of them, and the publications of the Henry Bradshaw Society are a monument (over fifty volumes) to their learning and industry. Some of this work has been prompted by a desire to search out the roots of the liturgy of the Church of England and some was prompted by the need to reform that liturgy. The Book of Common Prayer underwent reform right at its birth. The more Catholic First Book of Common Prayer (1549) was superseded by the edition of 1552 which at one time or another has been described as Calvinistic or Zwinglian. After the restoration of the monarchy in 1662 it was revised again though not fundamentally changed. From nearly the beginning of this century there have been several projects for reform which culminated in the appearance of the *Alternative Service Book* in 1980 which it is intended should exist alongside the Book of Common prayer. It would however take a very large volume to give some account of the liturgical scholarship and activity of the Church of England but two figures of this century have made notable contributions. Both are important as they influenced the reform that actually has taken place. They are Gabriel (Arthur) Hebert, SSM, and Gregory Dix, OSB.

In the Foreword by A. M. Allchin to a book called *Worship, Church and Society* by Christopher Irvine on the life and work of Gabriel Hebert we read: 'As the title of his best known book, *Liturgy and Society*, suggests, it was a vision of worship not as a specialised and limited activity, but as a focal point of human society as a whole. That is how Hebert envisaged the liturgy and if his view did not exhaust his interest in it yet it must be said that he always sought to relate liturgy to life'. That is what made him a pastoral liturgist even if the term was not in general use in England in his time. Though he was much else, a strong ecumenist and a noted Biblical theologian, that is what justifies his place in this book.

Gabriel Hebert SSM

Arthur Hebert born in 1886 into a clerical family of Huguenot descent, was educated at Harrow and New College, Oxford, where he read classics, philosophy and theology, gaining a first in the last. After pastoral work Hebert was ordained in 1912 and began his life at Kelham, the home of the Society of the Sacred Mission in 1913. There he was appointed theological tutor but almost immediately his work was interrupted by the outbreak of the 1914 war and Hebert was for some four years occupied with pastoral work. By 1920 he was in South Africa deeply involved in the Kelham mission there. He was professed as a brother of the SSM in 1921 and did some teaching. What was more important is that at the time he learnt his 'trade' as a pastoral priest serving two or three 'parish' centres and caring for great numbers of people. Two things relevant to our theme are notable. He designed a church and got it built (though unfortunately no description of it is given) and he drafted 'a series of services to celebrate the rites of the Christian initiation of adults' (p 15). This he would complete years later when he produced a liturgy remarkably like that of the current Roman rite which of course appeared long after his. The explanation of this is that the sources were much the same. Irvine's brief description of it is worth quoting: Hebert's 'draft initiation services... envisaged the restoration of the adult catechumenate, which provided a staged process of Christian formation, marked with liturgical celebrations, and enabled adults to make the transition from life in a pagan society to the life of faith in the Body of Christ, in a way which gave them sufficient time to appropriate that faith for themselves and feel that they belonged to the community of faith' (p 88).

It is not possible to trace the zig-zag course of Hebert's very busy life in any detail. He returned to England to teach at Kelham and from 1952 to 1961 he was professor of New Testament at Ormond College in Melbourne, Australia, and gave some lectures in the USA not long before he died in 1963.

What may surprise some is that this English Anglican priest was very much concerned with the Church of Sweden in the years before the Second World War. The Church of England had had relations with the Church of Sweden since the last decades of the nineteenth century. They felt they had much in common. In Sweden by the 1920s there was developing the movement symbolised by the *Högkyrka*, the 'High Church', which was rather different from what might seem to have been its counterpart in England. Between 1928 and 1961 Hebert made many visits to Sweden, he learned the language, translated among other things Gustaf Aulén's *Christus Victor* and gave many lectures. His main concerns were ecumenism and liturgy. He urged the practice of a weekly parish eucharist as the chief Sunday service, a practice with which he was already very familiar and which was also a foreshadowing of the Parish Communion he did so much to promote in England. In the liturgico-ecumenical field he found two snags. Much was (and is) made of confirmation in Sweden as a rite of passage about the time of adolescence but Hebert found that it was administered by a priest and not by a bishop and that there was no laying-on of hands! The Swedish church indeed had permanent deacons (which Hebert thought was a plus) but to his great surprise he found that they were not counted as 'clergy'.

Hebert became very well informed about Swedish theology and liturgy and he gives an interesting account of a eucharist celebrated in an ancient fourteenth century church at Malmö. First the celebrant in alb and stole conducted a kind of preparatory service consisting of hymn, address (about fifteen minutes) and a confession and absolution. He then returned to the sacristy and came back with another priest, both vested in green chasubles.[1] They approached the altar from either side and stood so that the communion vessels were visible to the people. There followed the *Sursum corda*, the preface, the institution narrative, the Lord's Prayer and then the Sanctus(!) After the Peace the communicants approached and knelt to receive. *After* the people had been communicated the two priests gave each other communion. The service ended with a prayer of thanksgiving and praise and the blessing.

The likenesses and unlikenesses with the Mass of the Roman rite will be noticed as also the influence of Luther, i.e. there was no *anamnesis* and no offering of any sort. In his later writings Hebert showed that he thought both of them were necessary.

It could be said, I think, that Herbert learnt his ecumenism in Sweden, though not exclusively. It was here at any rate that he was in dialogue with Swedish theologians like Bishop Söderblom, Brillioth and Aulén as well as with others in Denmark. Hebert was of the Anglo-Catholic wing of the Church of England but he never identified himself with it wholly. He thought that it was too often partisan and filled with a party spirit that was the antithesis of 'Catholic' and he constantly said that the true Catholic was also evangelical (if with a small 'e'!). His ecumenism was broad– but also deep. This can be illustrated by his welcome to Père Congar's *Chrétiens Désunis* (1953). Under the title 'Rome and Reunion' he wrote a review of the book in *Theology*. Seeing in it a sign that Roman Catholics were engaging in the ecumenical process, he also saw the book as a substantial contribution to the ecumenical debate because it emphasised the need for a soundly based theology of the Church, a theme Hebert had been stating for many years. He saw in the book a call for a clearer ecclesiology, 'that is, a systematic understanding of the nature and purpose of the Church', a question that Hebert himself tackled in his book *The Form of the Church*. But, although he did not live to see it, it was this that the Second Vatican Council provided in its Constitution on the Church (*Lumen Gentium*).

As he continued in his review, work for reunion was not to be regarded as a counterpart to the League of Nations. It was (and is) a theological task and only profound understanding of what 'Church' is can be the basis for a sound ecumenism (p 70).

It was this same understanding of the Church that underpinned so much of Herbert's writing on the liturgy. He was of course accustomed to a grave and dignified (and strongly sacramental) worship at Kelham and no doubt in Australia but he saw that ritual or, worse still, ritualism divorced from an understanding of 'Church' was superficial and did not get to the roots of the matter. His view is summed up in a by-line of Irvine's book: 'In worship above all the church is seen to be what it is' (p 77). Hebert came to this view through his own reflection and writing on the Church as the mystical body of Christ but he was greatly strengthened in his views by his contacts and visits to Maria Laach which under the influence of Abbot Herwegen and the 'mystery-theology' of Dom Odo Casel had become a centre for liturgical renewal in Germany. Here he both learnt and contributed. The mystery-theology, the making present in the liturgy of the saving work of Jesus Christ, appealed to him strongly and almost certainly influenced his insistence later that the eucharistic prayer must have an *anamnesis*, a dynamic recalling of the saving mystery, and also an element of offering. To this Hebert contributed from his deep Biblical knowledge the Hebrew notion of 'remembering', (*zikkaron*) which is also dynamic.

The effects of Hebert's contacts and discussion with continental liturgists became apparent in the Anglican move for liturgical revision later on. This is admirably summed up by Christopher Irvine: 'It would not be an exaggeration to say that Gabriel's visit to the Continental centres of the Liturgical Movement in the summer of 1932 was one of the most significant episodes of his whole life. For on this occasion the contacts and conversations he had with the monks of Mont-César and Maria Laach provided the inspiration for the greatest work of contributing to the renewal of the liturgical life of the Church of England, immediately prior to, and in a real sense of preparing the ground for, the era of liturgical revision and experimentation which began with the setting up of the Church of England's Liturgical Commission in 1955' (p 106).

The first result of these contacts was the book *Liturgy and Society* (1935) in which Hebert states that worship is the typical expression of the faith and doctrine of the Church, in other words, that the *lex orandi* is the *lex credendi* (the Church's prayer is the manifestation of its belief). It is also the manifestation of the Church understood as the mystical body of Christ, indwelt by the Holy Spirit, and the gathered people of God. He would have agreed with Dom Aidan Kavanagh that liturgy is the *Prima Theologia* (*On Liturgical Theology*, p 90, Pueblo, New York, 1984). A trained theologian himself, he yet saw that doctrine is not conveyed simply by rational discourse. The liturgy with its rites and symbols, with its images and poetry is a vehicle of divine truths that are needed by human beings (for we cannot comprehend God), and symbols and sacraments 'are subject to and controlled by the fact of the coming of God in the flesh, in history' (*Lit and Soc*, p 250). It was this connection of the liturgy with what I would call the incarnational process that led Hebert to emphasise the importance of Christian art especially as used in the liturgy. The Kelham chapel was a notable example of a dignified and, if one may use the word, uplifting art and architecture.

The second result of Hebert's contacts with the continent was the book, *The Parish Communion* (1937) which he promoted and edited, drawing on a number of authors whom he recruited. In the fourteen essays the authors laid out the importance of the eucharist as the centre of the Church's life and in practice urged that it should be placed as the principal act of worship of Sunday. As we know today, some six decades after the appearance of the book, the pattern in most Anglican churches is that urged by its author, principal among them of course Hebert himself. As Trevor Beeston has said, 'Few, if any collections of essays have had such a dramatic effect on the life of a church'. But once again his aim was not just to change (disturb) devotional habits. It was his desire and intention 'to set forth a conception of the nature of the Church, which appears to compel the adoption of the Parish Communion as its necessary expression in the liturgy. It is the idea of the Church that is primary' (p 124). He hoped that the parish Communion would not only manifest the Church (present in the local church) but would create or help to create community, Christian communities strongly bound together to resist among other things the dehumanising tendencies of Communism, Fascism and Nazism which faced and oppressed the Catholic Church all over Europe. In all this and much more his theology of the Church underpinned his view of active participation and what he wanted the liturgy to be for Anglicans, and as is obvious he anticipated the Second Vatican Council. Among other things, he was in favour of celebration in the 'westward position', i.e. facing the people, as it would emphasise community between clergy and people, and he experimented with concelebration. Influenced by what was going on in France he urged a somewhat elaborate form of 'offertory procession' but in this he exaggerated. The Order of the Roman Mass of 1970 played it down; the action is called the 'presentation of the gifts'.

Subsequently not all have been too happy about Hebert's views. The choral offices have suffered though it is doubtful whether the Morning Prayer, Matins, of the Book of Common Prayer, has the

attraction it once had. Others have been disturbed by the frequent communion of those who seem to receive without adequate
preparation. This is a concern for Roman Catholic pastors too and
the remedy seems to be a more adequate act of penitence in the
eucharistic liturgy and a better understanding and use of the
sacrament of Penance.

In the early 1920s the Church of England was much concerned
about the rite of Holy Communion and there was pressure for
change. There was much debate about the communion prayer
and many wanted to introduce an invocation of the Holy Spirit.
The debate came to a head with the proposed 1928 Prayer Book
which was thrown out by Parliament. If Hebert was not involved in that project at the time, as the debate continued he became dissatisfied with the proposals as they stood. There were
those who wanted to place the epiclesis immediately after the
words of institution and Gregory Dix did not want an epiclesis
of the Holy Spirit at all (he was too attached to the Roman
Canon). Hebert's ecumenical experience and theological insights, drawn from his many ecumenical encounters with East
and West, were broader than Dix's and more soundly based. He
insisted that a or the 'prayer of oblation' should be placed after
the words of institution to be followed by the epiclesis of the
Holy Spirit. To get around the objection that the epiclesis would
seem to be consecratory he even went as far as suggesting that
there might be an epiclesis before the words of institution. The
new eucharistic prayers of the Roman rite have also adopted this
solution!

In one way or another then Gabriel Hebert can be said to have
had a decisive influence on Anglican liturgical reform since 1957
and both before and after that date he had a very marked influence on Anglican liturgical practice. If the Anglican Eucharist
now looks very like the Mass or the Roman rite much of that
similarity is due to him.

Though fully aware of modern critical study of the Bible and although he used it, his intent was to search out and find the theological meaning of the Bible While accepting that there were
several 'theologies' in the Bible and also that the Hebrew Bible
must be allowed to deliver its own message or messages he
came strongly to emphasise the relationship between Old and

the New Testaments. he saw that the Old Testament was constantly pointing beyond itself, or to put it another way, that it was in a sense incomplete, and this was the theme of his most important book on the subject, *The Throne of David* (1941). It was thought to be so good that the Catholic Editions du Cerf had it translated into French when the war was over. To the *Throne of David* may be added his *Authority of the Old Testament* (1947). Above all he held that the Bible was the book of the Church and both the Old Testament and the New were shaped by worship[2] and by a *living* tradition, the handing on of the word throughout the ages by the Church.

Given all this, it is not surprising that Hebert saw that a sane typology was a key to the understanding of the Bible and indeed of the whole of salvation history; not surprising either that he saw the liturgy as the context for the reading and understanding of the Bible. As the French say, the Bible should be read 'en église'.

In conclusion I think it can be said that Gabriel Hebert was a forerunner of the liturgical movement which through his eyes can be seen to have been proceeding throughout the decades that preceded the Second Vatican Council. Its effects are now part of the life of the Roman Catholic Church and of the Church of England.

Bibliography

Christopher Irvine, *Worship, Church and Society*. An exposition of the work of Arthur Gabriel Hebert to mark the centenary of the Society of the Sacred Mission (Kelham) of which he was a member. Foreword by A. M. Allchin, Epilogue by Peter Hinchcliffe (The Canterbury Press, Norwich, 1993). From this book quotations in the above account are taken.

Dom Gregory Dix, OSB

Gregory Dix was a monk and it might seem that a monk was unlikely to make a contribution to liturgical practice though as the history of the Liturgical Movement illustrates many monks have done just that over the last one hundred and fifty years. They and he are examples of the importance of liturgical scholarship for an understanding of the liturgy and in the event of reform or revision, as the last fifty years have shown. Their learning has been a valuable and one would say an indispensable factor in the reshaping of liturgies. Too many have thought that they or anyone could monkey about with liturgies 'to make them popular' and if they had been let loose they would have destroyed them.

Gregory Dix (to give him his name in religion) was born in 1901 and educated at Westminster School and Merton College, Oxford, where he graduated in history. Ordained priest in 1925 he became a member of the Anglican Benedictine community at Pershore in Worcestershire and after some years teaching, joined that same community (which had moved to Nashdom in Bucks) where he was professed in 1940. From 1945 to 1952 he was prior and in that year came his early and much lamented death.

He wrote much, articles and reviews and several books. Here we can only consider three, the second two of which are by far the most important.

Gregory Dix ranged over a number of liturgical matters and in the middle 1930s he was much pre-occupied with Christian Initiation. Like many others since, he saw very clearly that baptism, confirmation and the eucharist were a unity but he developed a peculiar view of confirmation which may have been influenced by the standard practice of the Church of England at that time. He came to think that confirmation was theologically an *essential* part of initiation so that presumably without it a person is not quite a Christian. His view was that baptism is a prelude to confirmation and 'originated as the Christian equivalent of the circumcision imposed on proselytes to Judaism' and it was 'the effective rite of admission to the New Covenant'.[3] To back up his view he tried to show that everywhere in the New Testament that the word 'seal' is found it refers to confirmation. There seems to be no scripture scholar who agrees with him in this.

Later, in his *Theology of Confirmation* (1946) writing on the relation between baptism and confirmation he said that the baptism of water cleanses from sin and the 'sealing' (confirmation) confers the grace and gifts of the Holy Spirit.[4] Some colour can be given to this view by Tertullian (*De Baptismo* 6–8) but he has not been generally followed. He put this in a rather different way in the same book and I take it that it was intended to be an 'explanation' of his view: 'It is the Spirit who actually *operates* the salvation of each Christian, though the Spirit is shed forth only upon those united to the crucified and risen Christ by faith and regenerated and incorporated into him'. The term 'shed forth' is very vague and one is inclined to ask, Is not the Holy Spirit 'shed forth' in baptism also? It would seem that Dix has not been generally followed in this matter. Rejection of his views was sharply summed up by G.W.H. Lampe: 'If we are *in* Christ, we are *in* the Spirit' and by L. L. Mitchell (*Baptismal Anointing* (1966), p 189: Dix and others have 'perhaps been too ready to draw a sharp distinction between baptism in water and baptism of the Spirit and so destroyed that very unity for which they are contending'.[5]

I think it can be said that Dix earned his name as a scholar with his edition of the *Apostolic Tradition* of Hippolytus, a third century document that has had a more complicated history than almost any other. Its identity was revealed in 1916 by Dom Hugh Connolly, OSB, with his *The so-called Egyptian Church Order and derived documents* (Texts and Studies, Cambridge). It had to be dug out, so to say, from Arabic and Ethiopic collections and from the *Apostolic Constitutions* and the *Testament of our Lord*. It exists in a Latin text which is a translation from the Greek, made during the late fourth century or so. All these texts in various languages have to be marshalled, compared and critically examined, and that is what Gregory Dix did in his *The Treatise on the Apostolic Tradition of St Hippolytus of Rome* which appeared in 1937.[6] In view of the complexity of its history and the various kinds of expertise required in editing it, it was a notable feat of scholarship. In these circumstances there is room for much diversity of opinion and Dix formed his own. Even the identity of Hippolytus has been questioned but now it seems to be agreed that he was a Roman Greek-speaking priest (a rather irascible one) who differed with Pope Zephyrinus and his successor and went into schism. He died a martyr and is so honoured by the Church. This was Dix's view and he gives a lively account of him in his General Introduction, pp xii–xxxv.

The *Apostolic Tradition*, which was compiled about 215 AD, gives a unique insight into the liturgy and the religious life of

Christians at the time. It contains a collection of items about fasting, prayer, the *agapé* and some other matters (nos 22–41) but the most important part contains the author's account of the ordination of bishops, priests and deacons, the prayers by which they were ordained and a text of a eucharistic prayer which he proposes as a model that the new bishop might use, (1–14). Although the *Apostolic Tradition* had little or no impact on western liturgies it had a wide circulation in the East and, apart from the Latin version, all the others are in Greek or eastern languages. There it had considerable influence, an edition of it being found in the late fourth-century Greek *Apostolic Constitutions*. This influence is most notable in the prayer of the ordination of bishops which underlies all such prayers in the East until this day.

The re-discovery of the *Apostolic Tradition* in our own time has meant that it has had an extraordinary impact on the revision of current liturgies. Its ordination prayer is now the one used for the ordination of bishops of the Rome rite. The eucharistic prayer, heavily edited, appears as Eucharistic Prayer II in the Roman Missal of 1970 and another version of it is to be found in the Alternative Service Book, the Third Eucharistic Prayer. At least one reason for the popularity of this prayer with liturgical revisers is that this primitive text sets out in very simple form what must be described as the classical pattern of a eucharistic prayer. Likewise, the arrangement of the catechumenate in the *Order for the Christian Initiation of Adults* (RCIA) bears a close resemblance to the *Apostolic Tradition*, and the Liturgy of the sacraments of initiation, baptism, chrismation, confirmation and first eucharist is that of the Roman rite now in use (nos 15–21 in *Ap Trad*). It is an illustration of the importance of scholarly work and study in understanding and shaping the liturgy, even the liturgy we now have.

Gregory Dix was not only a liturgical scholar. It is interesting to find that in his contribution to Gabriel Hebert's *The Parish Communion*, he has a strong concern for the Church and for the people who make up the Church. Like Hebert, he reveals that all his concern for the liturgy is underpinned by the theology of the Church of which the celebration of the liturgy is the principal manifestation. Thus he wrote:

'The Eucharist is unmistakably the action and offering, not of the celebrant but *of the whole Church* in its hierarchic unity ....

So strong was the sense for the corporate offering of the
Eucharist that the Church was prepared to take risks to secure
it. St Cyprian can lay it down that when only a single presbyter
can be smuggled into the imperial prisons to celebrate for the
confessors awaiting martyrdom, he should be accompanied
by a deacon'.[7] He expands on this in chapters I and II of his
Shape of the Liturgy as well as elsewhere in that book.

So we come to Dix's most important work *The Shape of the
Liturgy* which was written during the Second World War and
was published in 1945. To strike a personal note, I remember
reading it with avidity and, like many others, being alternatively
delighted and exasperated by it. Dix was a provocative writer
and he often *meant* to provoke and occasionally he assumes an
olympian air; he is one who knows about these matters. What was
also exasperating is that although he was using and referring to
a vast amount of patristic literature only too rarely does he
annotate his remarks. Where I could check a few of his refer-
ences I found his translations sometimes said more than the
texts. Yet these are minor blemishes on a work that was im-
mensely creative, one which was read (and quarrelled with) all
over the world. Dean R.C.D. Jasper, who was for so many years
chairman of the Liturgical Commission of the Church of
England, could say this of *The Shape*: 'This book, despite its un-
tidiness, is a brilliant piece of work and has done more to stimulate
an interest in liturgy during the past twenty years than any
other work'.[8] To this one could add that Dix stimulated liturgical reform by making people think about liturgy and yes, its true
'shape'.

The Shape of the Liturgy which Dix himself called 'the Large Fat
Book', is just over 750 pages long and covers the development of
the liturgy from New Testament times, concentrating mostly on
the eucharist but also taking in the formation of the Liturgical
Year and the Divine Office. Here one can only deal with a few
points that have an interest of their own but which were also an-
ticipatory of much that was to come.

The merit of *The Shape* is that it called attention to the Jewish
meal which on the eve of the Sabbath had a special solemnity. In
the primitive Jewish-Christian church the eucharist was a
Jewish meal of some kind, the type to which it best conforms is

the formal supper of a *'chaburah...'* a fellowship meal, i.e. that of a 'brotherhood'. Scholars have rejected the *chaburah* but have largely accepted the 'meal' as the context of the Last Supper which would not then have been a Paschal meal though opinion on this matter is still undecided. Even if it was a Paschal meal, it was not that sort of meal that was repeated by the early Christians for the Pascha was celebrated only once a year but the 'breaking of the bread' was evidently celebrated frequently on the 'Lord's Day' in New Testament times.

Chaburah then can be dropped without detriment to Dix's views. What was of great and no doubt decisive importance in any discussion on the origins of the eucharist is the meal aspect which other scholars of various nationalities and church allegiances have accepted as crucial. The Jewish meal began with a 'blessing' over the bread (blessing practically = thanks to God for the gift of ...) which was broken and distributed. After the meal (see I Corinthians 11:25) there was the blessing of the cup, a long prayer and then the cup was passed round. It is generally held now that it was out of these two blessing prayers that there emerged the eucharistic prayer which is the nucleus and most important element of any Christian liturgy.

The second point we may notice is the replacement of the 'seven-action' pattern of the Last Supper by the 'four-section' pattern of the eucharist as it appeared in apostolic times. In the New Testament accounts Jesus took some bread, gave thanks, broke it and gave it to his disciples with what we call the 'words of institution'; then he took the cup, gave thanks again, gave it to his disciples saying certain words. Dix then states, 'With absolute unanimity the liturgical tradition reduces them to four' (p 48). These four are the *taking*, the *blessing*, the *breaking* and the *giving*. So far, so good. This is the basic 'shape'. But drawing out this pattern Dix made too much of the 'taking', seeing in it the 'offertory' with its procession. 'Taking' simply will not bear the weight put on it. In the earliest description of the eucharist (c 155), that of Justin the Martyr, the bread and wine are simply put on the table and then the president takes them. In the *Apostolic Tradition* deacons are described as bringing the bread and wine and placing them on the table. In the Roman rite of the eighth century (*Ordo Romanus Primus*) the pope with archdeacons and deacons *goes down* to the people, drawn up according to rank, and receives from them the offerings of bread and wine. In the Byzantine rite there is, it is true, an elaborate Great Entrance when the offerings are brought into with great ceremony. But in the Roman rite of 1970 the 'offertory' is played down. In the rite of 1570 it looked very much more like a 'sacrificial offering' (see the language of the fixed prayers) all on its own. Now, the 'offertory' is called 'The Presentation of the Gifts' or the Preparation. The Roman rite has made it clear that the true offering is made during the eucharistic prayer.

It may be too that Dix wanted to make too much of the 'breaking', the liturgical fraction of the bread before communion. It is true that 'the breaking of the bread' was one of the earliest titles of the eucharist (see Acts of the Apostles, to go no further) and that in I Corinthians 10:16, 17, the breaking of the one loaf is more than utilitarian; it is a symbol of the members of the (mystical) body of Christ all receiving from the one loaf which is his eucharistic body. But basically it was a utilitarian action to enable all in the assembly to receive from the one loaf. But this practice could not and did not last very long; the first communities were small. And to cite the Roman rite again, in eighth century Rome (and almost certainly before) in the papal Mass there were many loaves and to cover the breaking of them Pope Sergius I (+701) inserted the Agnus Dei. Wherever and whenever it is possible to use one altar bread from which all should communicate, it is of course highly desirable.

The 'giving', holy communion, provides no difficulties of interpretation though we note that the bread and wine are given one after another in the same rite.

The 'blessing' however is of immense importance. As we have suggested above, the 'blessing' in two parts was the 'thanksgiving', the eucharist, which in the Jewish culture was a blessing of God for, in this case, the gift of the bread and the wine, which became in the eucharist the body and blood of Jesus, the supreme gift. Since 1945 there has been an immense amount of research and scholarship devoted to this matter and it is now the general view that Dix's insights were correct. This is not to claim that Gregory Dix's view originated subsequent scholarship on the matter; that I think would be very difficult to prove but in this as in other matters he set people thinking about all the data that must be taken into account in the business of trying to establish how the liturgy of the eucharist came to be. Kenneth Stevenson however sums up as follows: 'Dix sees the origin of the eucharistic prayer in the Jewish *berakah* (the blessing prayer(s)), and this theory holds good, whatever happened at the Last Supper'[9] and he records that Pére Ligier recognises Dix's contribution although Ligier took it further.

Work on Hippolytus also led Dix to concern himself with the element of 'offering' within the eucharistic prayer which is found in the Text of the *Apostolic Tradition*. This has bee a bone of contention with some Anglicans but we need not consider that matter here. We are dealing with the views of Gregory Dix. He saw it as an essential element and since he and his community followed the Roman rite he was very familiar with the rich *anamnesis* (the *Unde et memores*) of the Roman Canon. Connected with this was indeed the question of the meaning of the *memoria*, the making the memory of the passion, death and resurrection and ascension of the Lord Jesus, an element that is found with only one or two exceptions in all the classical eucharistic prayers of the past. Here too, like Hebert, Dix recalled the meaning of the Jewish *zikkaron*, which does not mean a merely subjective 're-membering' of a past event but, as so respectable a document as the ARCIC ecumenical statement on the matter says, the memorial (i.e., making the memorial) was and is again understood as 'the making effective in the present of an event in the past' (section 5). The translators of the Roman Missal and the makers of modern liturgies of the eucharist have tried to bring this meaning out. Thus in the Roman Canon we read: 'Father, we *celebrate the memory* of Christ your son. We your people and your ministers, *recall* his passion ...'. Here again then it can be said that Dix was pointing the way to future liturgical reform.

In one matter Dix has not been followed. As has been indicated above, he had reservations about the epiclesis in the *Apostolic Tradition*. He held that it was an interpolation and in a long note in his edition of that document he attempts to justify his view of the matter.[10] Both the Roman and the Anglican liturgies have incorporated epicleses into their eucharistic prayers and both, I think it can be said, have gone beyond 'archaeological' considerations and have seen the theological rightness of the invocation of the Holy Spirit in the action of the eucharist.

If the above brief study of Dom Gregory Dix seems over-concerned with what might be called technical matters of interest only to other liturgists (though I do not think they are) it is well to remember that he contributed to Hebert's *Liturgy and Society* and saw very clearly that liturgy is concerned with life, the life of Christians and the life of society: 'We have forgotten that the study of liturgy is above all the study of *life*, that Christian worship has always been something done by real men and women, whose contemporary circumstances have all the time a profound effect upon the ideas and aspirations with which they come to worship'.[11] 'A study of life'; he may have learnt this from that 'pure' scholar, Edmund Bishop, who thought the same.

Notes

1. The chasuble was retained in Scandinavian countries after the Reformation. In Sweden and in the Domkyrka of Åbo in Finland there are collections of chasubles in the different styles from the late Middle Ages until the seventeenth century.

2. Subsequent scholarship on the Old Testament has justified Hebert's view.

3. See Kenneth Stevenson, *Gregory Dix, 25 years on*, Grove Books, Bramcote, Notts, 1970, p 4.

4. op cit p 5. His *Theology...*, p 10.

5. Both quotations as in Stevenson, pp 5, 7.

6. It was re-issued with corrections and an important preface and bibliography by Henry Chadwick in 1968.

7. Quotation in Stevenson, op cit, p 19. He could have added that when in southern Gaul the Church began expanding into the countryside the presbyter was always accompanied by a deacon.

8. Quoted in Stevenson, p 23.

9. op cit, p 25.

10. See *Apostolic Tradition*, 1937, pp 75ff and *The Shape of the Liturgy*, pp 157–162.

11. *The Shape ...*, p 741; quoted by Stevenson, op cit, p 35.

CHAPTER XII

Three Forgotten Liturgists

During the second half of the nineteenth century much scholarly work was being done in Germany and France and, as has been suggested above, by Anglican scholars in England. Among Catholics one can point only to Daniel Rock of whom a brief account has been given in a previous chapter. His older contemporary F.C. Husenbeth had indeed brought out a translation of the Roman Missal (1837) and a book for Sunday Vespers and he was a scholar in a rather old-fashioned way. But the standards of critical scholarship had been rising all through the nineteenth century, manuscripts were being discovered and others already known were being re-edited according to critical principles. The works of the Maurist monks in France, like Mabillon, were being appreciated anew and their editions and books were being brought into use again.

In all this work the English Catholic community played little part. It was too small, too poor and without any institute of higher learning. The Tractarian converts did something to raise the standard of secondary education among Catholics in England but they had neither the time nor it seems the inclination to engage in what were regarded as the obscure fastnesses of liturgiology. In the latter part of the century however, things began to improve and the names of Benedictines appeared: Aidan Gasquet, and rather later Cuthbert Butler and R. H. Connolly. The learned Herbert Thurston, SJ, was a nineteenth century man as was also the polymath Adrian Fortescue. All these were priests but among them was a layman, Edmund Bishop who eventually was acknowledged to be one of the most learned liturgical scholars of his time.

It may be asked, what had these men and others to do with the liturgical movement which is above all a practical affair? Like their continental counterparts they were discovering the origins and true shape of the liturgy and themselves coming to a better understanding of it, knowledge that they passed on to those who would read them. It is true to say that had there not been these many decades of scholarly investigation (that incidentally went on right up to Vatican II and still continues) the liturgical movement would have been infinitely more difficult and might have foundered altogether. For there were those who fifty or more years ago held tenaciously to the view that the Roman rite of 1570 was sacrosanct, that to all intents and purposes it was perfect, and must not be touched. There were those who thought that the Mass in Rome (they knew nothing of the eastern liturgies) had always been in Latin, that the Mass as they knew it had been celebrated in the catacombs, that excrescences like the Last Gospel had always been there, and so on. What was more important, most people thought that the right attitude to the Mass was one of reverent silence; they had no active part in it, even though the celebrant (who had his back to them) occasionally addressed them. Thanks to the work of the scholars it gradually impinged on people that the Mass is the act of a community in which they have a part to play. To this work these three liturgists made their contribution.

Edmund Bishop

Of the three Edmund Bishop was by far the most important as a 'pure' scholar. He spent the greater part of his life in scholarly pursuits, he never held any official position in the Church and incidentally the Church did not choose to acknowledge or reward his labours.[1] He was an autodidact and had to wait long for any recognition from his peers.

Edmund Bishop was born in 1846, the seventh child of Michael and Susan Bishop. His parents had been in service in the household of the Duke of Somerset, near Totnes in South Devon. He set them up in Seymour Hotel and perhaps understandably, Edmund's biographer calls the father an 'innkeeper'. In fact, the family seem to have been in easy circumstances and the mother, though much occupied with bringing eight children into the world, was a cultivated woman though largely self-educated. She used to read large extracts from Shakespeare's plays to her children as well as other writers. Edmund went to two grammar schools, in the second of which at Ashburton he was very well taught. Like two of his elder brothers he was sent to Belgium, to Vilvorde near Brussels, for the rest of his formal education. He spent two years there, was again well taught and he became practically bi-lingual. Thanks to his mother (she died in 1864) who sought the help of the Duke for Edmund, he, after examination, became Third Class clerk in the Department of Education. It was an easy if boring job; the hours of work were (until the Education Act of 1870) from 11.00am to 5.00pm. The salary was £100 per annum, rising eventually to £340. In 1885 he retired on a pension of £175. I give these financial details to show that Bishop had enough to live on (a family could exist on £1 a week at the time and many had less) though he was never wealthy. He had enough however to amass an important scholarly library (now with his papers at Downside Abbey), the pound sterling was hard currency and he could afford foreign books. He earned something eventually by his writings but it can never have been much.

In appearance Bishop was tall and thin, often ailing (bad colds) and he grew a luxuriant beard. His manners were courtly and his excellent 'library manners' won him the ready attention and, it seems, the affectation of librarians from the British Museum to the Bibliothéque Nationale and the Vatican Library. Though a most painstaking scholar, an exact paleographer and a student of a wide range of history, especially medieval, his life was anything but tranquil. He lived in many places, he 'tried his vocation' as a monk at Downside (which proved to be a false move) and had to transport his ever-growing library from one dwelling place to another. For a time he lived with Dom Aidan Gasquet and another monk in London and for several years assisted Gasquet in his researches. He assisted him in his book *Henry VIII and the English Monasteries* (1888–9) which had a great *réclame*, as well as other books, for example *Edward VI and the Book of Common Prayer*, Bishop doing the most important part of the work. Indeed, it has been said that when Bishop ceased to assist Gasquet the latter earned the notoriety of being anything but an accurate scholar. In fact, Bishop gave similar service to a great number of other scholars and rather dissipated his efforts. He was excessively scrupulous about accuracy himself and often found it difficult to make absolute statements. This made it impossible for him to produce a large scale work and also affected his style, which was full of qualifications though at his best, when he was confident, he could write flowingly and well. His 'remains' were gathered together by himself with the assistance of Dom Hugh Connolly and were published in the massive volume *Liturgica Historica* (OUP, 1918) a year after his death.

How then did Edmund Bishop contribute to the liturgical movement? It has to be said at once that for the most part he did so only indirectly. He was among those at the time who discerned the true shape of the original Roman rite. In use was the *Missale Romanum* in the edition of 1570 and in the nineteenth century (for the Maurists' work had been forgotten or was disregarded) most people thought that it was the Mass Book of the ancient Roman Church. In fact it was the missal as Charlemagne had propagated it in his dominions in the eighth and ninth centuries (c 795 to 814). He wanted a uniform liturgy in his empire, the see of Rome ranked high in his thinking and for him it was the only source from which he could obtain an authentic book of the Roman rite. This he sought from Pope Hadrian I and when it arrived (c. 785-6) he and his advisers realised (somewhat to their dismay, we may imagine) that it was a sacramentary containing the papal liturgy. It provided only for those times and occasions when the pope celebrated *solemniter*, i.e. roughly, from Advent to Pentecost. There was nothing for the Sundays after Pentecost (as they came to be called in the ninth century) and other things were missing too. The book had to be supplemented and a large supplement was duly added, as it is now thought by Benedict of Aniane though in Bishop's time it was thought to be by the English monk, Alcuin.[2] In the first editions the supplement was carefully marked off from the original material, the supplement beginning with the word *Hucusque*, 'Up to this point' (you have the Roman sacramentary). Later copyists left this out with the consequence that in later centuries everyone thought that the whole of the *Missale Romanum* had come from the hand of Gregory the Great.

Bishop spent years investigating this matter, some of the results of which can be seen in his article 'The Earliest Roman Mass Book' in *Liturgica Historica* (pp 39–61) which in fact is mostly concerned with the so-called Gelasian Sacramentary. In the same collection will be found 'On Some Early Manuscripts of the Gregorianum' and 'On Some Early Texts of the Roman Canon', both of which require very close reading. The purpose of citing them here is that they and other studies of Bishop on the origins of the Roman liturgy were the source of his one undoubtedly popular booklet 'The Genius of the Roman Rite'. It is rightly the first essay in the collection *Liturgica Historica* (pp 1–19). It was widely read, it was translated into French and it was influential. It was a work of *haute vulgarisation* which brought to the knowledge of many an understanding of the 'Roman-ness' of the Mass of the Roman rite that few had before. To do this he had to separate out from the missal as it was those elements that were truly Roman and those that were not. He was able to do this thanks to his prolonged study of the early sacramentaries, including the *Hadrianum* which Hadrian I had sent to Charlemagne, as well as the MS of Cambrai which Bishop ranked high.

To make his point clear he lists first the non-Roman elements and then the Roman. The former include the psalm *Iudica* (and the confession that followed), the prayers at the 'offertory' (seven in all) which he described as French (though some were in fact of Spanish provenance) and the private prayers of the priest before communion. The Roman elements are the collect, the epistle and the gospel, the 'proper' prayer over the offerings, everything from the Preface-Canon to the communion, and the post-communion prayer and the dismissal. To illustrate the difference in 'genius' or spirit between Roman and texts from elsewhere he compares the Roman Preface for the Mass of Pentecost with that in a Spanish or Mozarabic missal; the first is but eight lines which say all that is necessary, the Spanish text is eighty lines and, as Bishop remarks, goes winding on until one has lost the thread. He give examples of collects and what are now called presidential prayers said (sung) by the celebrant, points out their brevity and sobriety and contrasts them with other Gallican prayers which are much longer. The differences are marked but were little noticed before Bishop's time. Summing up he says that the genius of the Roman rite is 'soberness and sense'.

For Bishop the study of liturgy was not just a study of texts and rites. It was a study of religion or what we could call devotion which has been called in more recent times 'religiosity', though not in a pejorative sense. What were (and are) people's fundamental religious attitudes and how were these expressed in actions and eventually in words and rites? It was because of this (and in it Bishop was much in advance of his time) that he made no harsh judgement on the non-Roman elements that had attached themselves to the Roman stock. He saw them as the necessary expressions of peoples, German and French, north of the Alps whose religious-psychological needs were different from the Romans or at any rate the Roman clerics who for four centuries had been writing prayers for the Mass and indeed for the Divine Office. There is every sign however that Bishop himself preferred that more ancient Roman tradition though he did not proclaim his preference publicly.

He was also aware that liturgy had to develop or die and when he came to consider later eucharistic devotions he does so quite calmly. It was in this context that he initiated a view that became a thesis for some. From the evidence he had he believed that the Exposition of the Blessed Sacrament and Benediction had their origins not in Italy (where most people looked for them) but in Germany and the Low Countries where in fact the cult of the Blessed Sacrament exposed began, this being sanctioned by the Pope in 1264 with the institution of the Feast of Corpus Christi and the very limited permission for Exposition. To back up his views he refers to four articles by Herbert Thurston in *The Month* (June-September, 1901).

Bishop's view was turned into a thesis by Gregory Dix who in *A Detection of Aumbries* (1942) as well as elsewhere, maintained that there was something that he called 'Northern Catholicism'. His thesis was that *all* in the Roman rite that was thought to be typically Roman Catholic and stemming from Italy had in fact come from France, the Low Countries and Germany. As so often he wanted to *épater le bourgeois*, that is, the more conventional Anglicans who did not like 'Italian devotions'. Edmund Bishop did not like exaggerated views; he would not I think have endorsed those of Gregory Dix. A more balanced and well-documented account of the matter will be found in Nathan Mitchell, OSB, *Cult and Controversy: The Worship of the Eucharist Outside Mass* (Pueblo Publishing Company, New York, 1982).

If it be asked whether Bishop made any direct contribution to the liturgical movement of his time it has to be said first that he was deeply attached to the Benedictines and played an important part in the restoration of full monastic observance at Downside in which he was the constant collaborator of Dom Aidan Gasquet (later Cardinal). Bishop's knowledge of Benedictinism was deep and extensive and he put it at the disposal of Gasquet and those who supported him. Bishop loved to worship at Downside and spent much time there but he was also a parishioner in several different parishes. He made no fuss, he attended Mass devoutly and in his last place of residence at Barnstaple he had a high regard for the parish priest and very friendly relations with him. From one or two casual remarks it seems that Bishop did not think liturgical reform was possible or even perhaps desirable. In accordance with his views on the development of worship in which for him the *people* played an important role he was probably ready to wait for some sort of development that would be stimulated from below rather than imposed from above. There is a sense in which this happened though priests and monks as well as some laypeople worked for an improved participation and, as everyone knows, brought about a liturgical reform mandated by the Second Vatican Council. Authority finally sanctioned what had been desired by a very widespread movement in the Church.

Yet in one or two matters Bishop was able to make a contribution. It was the time of the designing and building Westminster Cathedral and Bishop was able to put at the disposal of Bentley, the architect, his vast knowledge of church architecture in the matter of the *baldacchino* over the high altar. It is not clear whether he liked the new cathedral. Of it he wrote: 'My summing up of the building is that it spells ... the end of that romanticism which has carried so many of us to 'Rome' and a good many to 'Romanism'... though what he meant by that is not clear. He had become a Catholic in 1867 at the age of twenty-one when I suppose the 'Goths' were triumphant.[3]

It is understandable that he should have been interested when Cardinal Vaughan canvassed the somewhat romantic and impracticable notion that a community of Benedictines should live at the cathedral and maintain the choir offices and presumably the whole of the liturgy. It came to nothing. Bishop was also interested personally when after the death of Vaughan it became known that of the three names on the *terna*, two of them were Benedictines, his friend Cardinal Gasquet and Bishop Cuthbert

Hedley, also a Benedictine. He knew Gasquet very well and yet was not certain he would be right for Westminster but after consideration he thought he would be the best man for England. In the event Francis Bourne, Bishop of Southwark, was appointed and though this was a disappointment, Bishop was not incommoded by him in any way.

Unlike many liturgists before and since Bishop was very concerned about the Divine Office and its celebration. He collaborated heavily with Dom Switbert Bäumer on his *Geschichte des Breviers* (1895). He was a man who was truly scholarly, one with whom Bishop could work very happily. The book also gave him an opportunity to correct the errors and unsupported theories of P. Batiffol in his *Histoire du Bréviaire Romain* (1895). As Bäumer himself was aware, the time had not yet come for a definitive history of the 'breviary' (i.e. the Divine Office) and that history has not been definitively written to this day.

All of this was at a scholarly level and at the level of practice there is one curious incident. With his friend Everard Green he was invited by the unfortunate St George Mivart (who later on died outside the Church) to support an effort at a liturgical revival in the church of St Charles, Ogle St, London, where the parish priest Fr Regan was amenable. The propositions were that there should be daily recitation of the Divine Office, and that the standard of liturgical music should be improved. The attempt came to nothing. As with so many things Mivart touched, controversy ensued by which time Bishop had withdrawn from the scheme. The proposal however shows that Bishop would have like to restore the celebration of the Divine Office in parish churches wherever it was feasible.

These are details however. Edmund Bishop was distinguished by his great scholarship and the stimulation and help he gave to others. His rank as a scholar on the continent is indicated by the tribute of another scholar, a Byzantinist, Comte Paul Riant. Writing to Fr Antrobus of the London Oratory in 1880 he said that Bishop, in his opinion, was a first class scholar '... he has an enormous fund of knowledge, a very reliable and keen critical sense, a great ability for hard work, combined with an imperative need for minute accuracy. In him there is the stuff of a Montfaucon or a Mabillon'.[4] This last remark would have pleased Bishop greatly if it had ever come to his knowledge. He had a great regard for the Maurist monks of the seventeenth and eighteenth centuries and esteemed their work very highly.

Bibliography

The Life and Work of Edmund Bishop (1959) by Nigel Abercrombie who provided a very full and detailed biography of Edmund Bishop with assessments of much of his work. The book however would have benefited from a chronology as Bishop moved about so much and was involved in so many schemes that it is difficult to find out where he was and what he was doing at any given time.

Among the more 'popular' articles in *Liturgica Historica* the following may be mentioned: The Origins of the Feast of the Conception of the Blessed Virgin Mary (Anglo-Saxon England, only Naples coming before); The Origins of the Cope as a Church Vestment (not a eucharistic vestment as some wanted to maintain); Of Six Candles on the Altar (how they got there); Pastor Dreygerwolt's Note-Book (one source of the 'Northern Catholicism' theory).

Adrian Fortescue

Fortescue was not a 'professional' liturgist if by that term is meant one who devotes his whole life to the study of liturgy. He was a pastoral priest, though a rather unusual one, of the Archdiocese of Westminster and the founder of the church of Letchworth in Hertfordshire. He was a very learned man and a priest who put his knowledge at the service of others.

Born in 1874, after schooling in France and at St Charles's College, Bayswater, he went off to Rome, entered the Scots' College to read for the Ph.D (1899). Not liking Rome very much, it seems, he went for his theology to the University of Innsbruck where after some six years of study he gained two doctorates in theology and Church History. He passed with distinction in Hebrew and Arabic.

Fortescue was a considerable linguist; apart from the usual Greek and Latin, he had Italian, German (his second language), Hungarian (that very difficult language), Sanscrit, Icelandic as well as modern Greek. He was well prepared for his travels. In 1906 he obtained leave of absence for one year and spent it in the Near East, Beirut being his base. It was here and at this time that he began to write his book, *The Orthodox Eastern Church* (1908). To this at this point may be added his *Lesser Eastern Churches* (1913) and the *Uniate Churches* (1917) which he did not live to complete. In spite of some unpleasantly polemical writing in the first of these books, Fortescue shows a real understanding of the Eastern Churches and from his meticulous descriptions of their liturgies a liking for them and their ways. He was certainly the foremost authority in England on those churches at the time. His descriptions of the liturgies also bear witness to his strong interest in the subject and to a knowledge of them that was rare in the west at the time. He also propagated a knowledge and an experience of the Byzantine Liturgy by arranging a celebration of it according to the rite of St John Chrysostom in Westminster Cathedral in 1908.

In 1907 he was appointed to Letchworth and at first said Mass in a hut near the railway but by 1908 he had got his church built and by 1909 a house to live in. It was during this very busy time that he began his book, *The Mass, A Study of the Roman Liturgy* which was published in 1912.[5]

It is important to note that Fortescue was writing a manual for the diocesan clergy. He was not writing a book of primary scholarship on a subject, the Mass, which was and still is, a highly complicated subject. Edmund Bishop refused to read it, perhaps out of pique or wounded by the knowledge that one who was not an acknowledged liturgical scholar should have taken upon himself (in fact he was invited by the editor of the series) to write an account of the Roman Mass. Yet, as one goes through it, one finds that it is fact very learned; his account of the liturgy (or liturgies) as it can be discerned in the Church Fathers of the second and third centuries has stood the test of time and is very well worth reading today. In any case, it was the first scholarly history of the Mass of the Roman rite in English and greatly in advance of anything available to the English clergy before. It was liked and approved of by that very critical scholar Herbert Thurston and it was widely read for over forty years. Understandably various parts of it are out of date; since he wrote there have been seventy years of scholarly research,

many questions have received an answer and if even now light
has not been thrown on every detail, the main lines of the history
of the Mass of the Roman rite are clear. Father J. A. Jungmann,
the distinguished author of *Missarum Sollemnia* (1948), perhaps
recalling that Fortescue was an old alumnus of Innsbruck,
thought *The Mass* was sufficiently important to include in his
bibliography.

Fortescue wrote other things on the liturgy, a pamphlet on the
ample form of the chasuble which he introduced into his church
and was followed by many others though Rome disapproved
(vainly) in 1925. He wrote an essay *Concerning Hymns*, another
on the Rites of Holy Week and revised the *English Missal* (1915)
which in fact was a revision and partial re-translation of the
missal of F.C. Husenbeth of 1837.[6] The book however that made
Fortescue a household name for decades, up to the time of the
Second Vatican Council was *The Ceremonies of the Roman Rite
Described* which first appeared in 1917. It was already in a third
edition by 1920, it remained in print (and constant use) until it
was brought up to date and re-edited by Canon J. B. O'Connell
(who however at one point replaced Fortescue's attractive drawings with full chasuble (a sign of priest-celebrant) with one of
the Roman shape). Little could he have seen the very long life
and prestige of his book which, it appears, was written for
money (£100) to help him pay his bills at Letchworth.[7] Fortescue
had no special interest in ceremonial and it is not surprising that
in the first edition he made mistakes. These annoyed some of the
experts but what annoyed them a great deal more was what they
construed as 'anti-Romanism' in the book which would be better
described as 'anti-Italianism'. Thus, for Fortescue Latin was the
official language of the Church, not Italian, and he objected to
the intrusion of Italian words when there were plenty of good
Latin words for certain things. Thus the hand-candlestick that
used to be held when a bishop was reciting a prayer from a book
had come to be called a *bugia* (which awkwardly in Italian can
mean a 'lie') became a *scotula*. There was less justification for
latinising certain Italian terms: the cape once worn by monsignori, the *mantella* became the *mantellum*. And so on. What
however infuriated many of the clergy (often Roman trained)
andMCs was Fortescue's mocking of the existing books of ceremonial. He saw his book as replacing one called the 'Dale-
Baldeschi' which was a circumlocutory translation of the Italian.

This he mercilessly mocked. What was worse, he had rude things to say about the cumbersome work on ceremonial by one Martinucci which was regarded by most MCs as their 'bible'. Reading it, Fortescue averred, it was rather like travelling in a slow stopping train at stations without a name so that you never knew where you were. Finally, in describing the various ranks of clerics and their roles in celebration from cardinals downwards he came to the then various degrees of monsignori and here he gave up. As star differs form star in glory, he wrote, so does one monsignor differ from another. The whole of his introduction is one of the wittiest pieces of writing of the time, it is marvellous prose and for most very amusing. The *conoscenti*, as I have said, were furious and Fortescue was very unpopular in some quarters. In later O'Connell editions it was withdrawn – much to my regret.

The above are only a few of Fortescue's literary efforts and all the time he was a busy parish priest. His church of St Hugh was blessed with the celebration of High Mass 6th September 1908 and was followed by the celebration of the Byzantine liturgy (eucharist) with Fortescue singing the responses. Never before or since has any church in this country, I imagine, been opened in such fashion. On the following Christmas Eve Matins of the Divine Office was sung before Midnight Mass and presumably Lauds after it, as the Roman rite then laid down. By January of the next year Compline was sung. Fortescue not only had the people participating in the celebration of the liturgy but he taught them its meaning. He wrote a booklet *Sunday Vespers*, he edited another on what he called the great Latin hymns of the church and he arranged it so that on one page there was the Latin text with chant and on the facing page a translation in English *so that all could understand* what they were singing. By April of 1909 the liturgy of Holy Week was celebrated in full, including the offices of Tenebrae. He tended his choir carefully, writing music for them, teaching them plainsong (to be sung according to his own theory!) and, with his servers, prepared the liturgy of the great feasts, especially the great days of Holy Week, with care. His sermons were short and full of meat and those on the Passion of our Lord at the evening services of the Sundays of Lent drew large crowds which included many who were not Catholics. In the terms of the time, he made many converts and as might be expected, instructed them thoroughly. As

Dr Vance said in his funeral sermon on him, his was the best educated congregation in Europe!

The little church was a model of it kind , simple yet warm. The altar was properly dressed with frontals (according to the colours of the liturgical year) on which were Greek designs, and over it was a *ciborium* (a canopy, as the rubrics required, *not* to be called a *baldacchino*). The vestments were of the old medieval design, notably the ample chasuble– and Fortescue wrote a tract on those too, illustrated with a drawing of the chasuble of St Thomas Becket.

But Fortescue was not a ritualist. All he did was in his own view simply practical, that which was required by a proper and de-vout celebration of the liturgy, what indeed was required by the rubrics of the then Roman rite which some chose to neglect. Nor was the liturgy something merely for the clergy. It belonged to the people as well and they were invited to celebrate it in full, Divine Office and all. Moreover, he extended his pastoral care not only to his own people but to all who came to him, to all who sought his help. His relationships with the neighbouring Anglican clergy seem to have been good– he studied Hebrew with some of them! – and when preaching on the English martyrs he remembered the Protestant martyrs 'who also died for what they conceived to be the truth'.

When the first World War came he was busy with refugees and preached in French and Flemish, as well as English, on Sundays and published his notices in all three languages.

To bring this chronicle to an end, all that remains to be said that in 1919 he was made *Consultor of the Congregation Pro Ecclesia Orientali* and appointed professor of Church History at St Edmund's College, Old Hall, Ware, an appointment that gave him great pleasure. He was a most acceptable member of staff and in moments of relaxation had them rolling with laughter as he told his stories, mimicking people in several languages. His work in his parish, where he continued to reside, went on, he still lectured on a variety of subjects here and there and in 1922 spent his last holiday in Bavaria and his beloved Tyrol. On his return his work continued as usual, he wrote on the 'Church in Malabar' for the *Cambridge History of India*, he continued his lec-tures and then towards the end of December he visited his doc-

tor who referred him to a consultant in London who diagnosed
cancer. Fortescue went back to his beloved church, celebrated
the Christmas liturgy and on 31 December he preached his last
sermon on 'Christ our Friend and Comforter'. He left his church
kissing the *mensa* of the altar, on 3 January and after two oper-
ations, died on 11 February 1923, at the early age of 43. His death
was a sad loss to the Church and to his many friends. But his
work continued after him. He had disciples whom perhaps he
did not know; during his busy life he had stimulated and encouraged many and if there was no one to continue his scholarly
work his books lived on and instructed them.

Bibliography

Adrian Fortescue. A Memoir. By John G. Vance and J. W.
Fortescue (1924). This is a very elegantly produced book, one of
the best at the time when Burns and Oates were producing beautiful
books, including Fortescue's *Ceremonies of the Roman Rite*. There is a
brief and lively evocation of Fortescue as parish priest by Edith
Cowell in *Blackfriars*, Vol IV, no 41, August 1923. One could have
wished that someone before now would have written a full scale
biography. There are not only Fortescue's many publications but
also texts of his many lectures and it seems a considerable number of
letters which may contain criticisms of persons and things but
which could well be published now.

Herbert Thurston, SJ

In the earliest decades of this century Herbert Thurston gained
for himself something of the reputation of an iconoclast or, to
use a more vulgar term, a debunker of the pious legends that
had disfigured the saints for centuries. Their humanity had
almost disappeared from view, they were perfect, sometimes
even from birth, and in the conventional literature of the Middle
Ages they had become little more than pegs on which to hang
virtues. In this work Thurston was the disciples and student of
the Bollandist Fathers who from the early seventeenth century
began searching out the authentic documents on which to build
their massive *Acta Sanctorum* which now consists of a long series
of volumes from the month of January onwards. As scientific
historiography made new demands in the nineteenth century,
so the Bollandists stepped up the critical standard of their work,

largely represented in their *Analecta Bollandiana*. Among other things they examined critically the *acta* of the early martyrs, put them into different categories ranging from contemporary records to the *legenda* (something to be read– in the Divine Office or even at Mass) which had been composed by monks of, say, the seventh, or even later centuries and who can have had no access to original information. Thus St Cecilia who came to be associated with music on the strength of a phrase in her legend *cantantibus organis*, became the partoness of music, as she still is. There is no evidence of this at all. A Cecilia was a martyr but there is nothing to say that she was a virgin as she appears in our calendar to this day. This and similar strippings of saints of their traditional legends upset great numbers of pious people as did more recently the refusal of church authorities to accept any longer that any such saint as Philomena had ever exixted.[8]

All this may seem very negative but clerics and scholars since the sixteenth century had objected to and even ridiculed the presence of baseless legends of the saints in the Divine Office (the famous or infamous 'second nocturn'). The historian Baronius had cautiously made a few changes in that same century at the request of the pope but the legends remained substantially what they were. Complaints continued through the centuries (voiced at Vatican I, 1870) but it was not until the Roman Calendar of 1969 and the revised Office of 1971 that a remedy, and a complete one, was found. Instead of a 'legend' the office of a saint is prefaced with a brief notice of his or her life containing such facts as are available. The *lectio* or reading is taken either from an authentic source (e.g. the official account of the martyrdom of St Cyprian), or from a contemporary biographer or from the writings, if any, of the saints.

Thurston, of course, was not connected with this but it can be said that with his Bollandist confrères he prepared the way. In this field of study his most important work was the revision, which in his hands was a radical revision, of the famous Butler's *Lives of the Saints* which had been written in the eighteenth century by Alban Butler, a recusant priest. For its time it was respectable, and respected, widely owned and perhaps ready by generations of Catholics. In about 1920 Thurston took on this task, largely re-writing according to modern principles of hagiography all the entries from January to December. He retained what he could of

Butler's work, though it is not very visible, and he had to write biographies of the many saints who had been canonised or beatified since the eighteenth century. The work was arduous and first he recruited Norah Leeson to help him and finally Donald Attwater who completed the work in twelve volumes. Later it was published as four volumes and Michael Walsh, the Librarian at Heythrop College, has continued the work in one way or another.

Thurston's Butler's *Lives* is a work of sound scholarship and a very reliable reference book. It is possible that it is now not used as much as it once was since in the last twenty-five years interest in the saints has waned somewhat. However, Thurston and his colleagues set a standard that has been the basis of modern hagiography, greatly to the benefit of the saints themselves.

His principle work on liturgy was *Lent and Holy Week – Chapters on Catholic Observance and Ritual*, which was published in 1904. The date is not unimportant. The scholarly research of Edmund Bishop has been proceeding for many years by this time, as had the work, of French scholars like Louis Duchesne and of German scholars. Thurstaon was aware of it, he urged Bishop to get on 'with the sacramentaries' and he approved of Fortescue's The Mass to which he added 'A Supplementary List of Books' in the 1930s.

Lent and Holy Week was a work of genuine scholarship, the only historical account of the complicated liturgies of that season that, as far as this writer knows, existed at that time. In discreet footnotes he reveals his knowledge of patristic literature, medieval sources of various kinds and the modern secondary literature that had been appearing for some years. It is also full of much recondite information that does not appear in modern histories of the liturgy. Thurston's erudition was indeed very extensive. It will be obvious however, from the date of publication, that parts of the book will have been superseded by later research. Given the state of knowledge at the time, it is not surprising that Thurston did not always realise that there was a distinction between what was done in the church in Rome and what was done north of the Alps. The whole elaboration of the Palm Sunday rite is not found until we come to the tenth century with the appearance of the Romano-German pontifical. The procession and the build up of a ministry of the word like that of the first part of the Mass, and the veneration of the Gospel book and later of the Blessed Sacrament are all transalpine practices. Though he is aware of the origin of the veneration of the Cross on Good Friday (it is Byzantine) he does not connect it with the Syro-Greek popes of the time and does not give a description of the very austere papal rite. He is of course aware of the anomaly of celebrating a night service (the Easter Vigil) in the morning: 'It is difficult to persuade oneself at eight o'clock on Saturday morning that the sun has already set, that our watch (vigil) is nearly over, that more than twenty-four hours have elapsed since our Blessed Lord was laid in the tomb'. Referring to the ninth/tenth liturgical writers he repeats their injunction that the Gloria of the Easter Vigil Mass should not be sung 'until the stars begin to appear'. At the same time, he seems to think that the Vigil Service is not quite the celebration of Easter, or rather of the whole redeeming work of Christ from his death to his resurrection. These shortcomings are perfectly understandable. Thurston was conditioned by his own time and experience though we may suspect that he would have been happy to see a night Vigil restored to night!

From the viewpoint of this brief study the above details are not of primary importance. One would not read Thurston's book for an up to date account of the complicated history of Lent and Holy Week though there is much here that is not found in many modern books on the subject (e.g., it is very difficult to find an explanation of Laetare Sunday and its observances in them). Thurston makes a disclaimer in his preface to write a devotional book yet as one goes through it, it is clear that he had a great love of the liturgy. He writes persuasively, evidently desiring that his readers shall be moved by the depth of meaning and yes, devotion in the texts. These he translates and frequently comments on pointing out their spiritual value. He quotes passages from the poems of Canon Oakley to illustrate and deepen people's understanding of text and season. Although even by his own brethren he was regarded as near sceptical in some matters, here and surprisingly often, he presents some of his conclusions with due reservation and evidently with the intention of not upsetting anyone. Occasionally he lets fly. Writing of the folded chasuble and broad stole (formerly used in Lent and Advent) he refers with distaste to the cutting down of the chasuble which had 'grown and grown until at last we have reached the fiddle-pattern card-board lined abomination, the modern French chasuble' (pp 161–2).

In another place (p 240, fn 1) he speaks of the liking or even the love the laity had for the Divine Office in the Middle Ages; they attended Matins (which included Lauds), Mass and Evensong (Vespers) in their parish churches and, as Thurston knew well enough though he does not refer to the matter here, they complained on the occasion of parish Visitations if their parson did not recite the offices or skimped them. He also laments that the Marquis of Bute's translation of the Divine Office had been allowed to go out of print and tried to do something to fill the gap by publishing with the Catholic Truth Society translations of the Office of Tenebrae. In another place he expresses that 'the solemn daily chanting of the Divine Office (has now been) happily inaugurated in Westminster Cathedral' (p 238).

An unusual feature of a book on the liturgy of Lent and Holy Week is that Thurston investigated a number of practises and popular devotions connected with the season. Thus he discourses on the obscure question of the Lenten Curtain (which has some connection with the veiling of images in Passiontide); in the Middle Ages it hung in chancels hiding the altar or in parish churches, before the chancel itself. The explanation of the practice seems to be that in Lent, a time of repentance, all Christians are regarded as sinners and at least temporally excluded from the 'Holy of holies'. He also discusses the origin of the *Quarant' Ore*, the Forty Hours Prayer before the Blessed Sacrament that usually took place about Passiontide. He traces it to Milan in 1537, and its propagation to St Charles Borromeo, Archbishop from 1564 to 1584. More recent research has uncovered a slightly earlier example. One A. Belotti in 1527 in a Lenten sermon urged the people to pray before the Blessed Sacrament for forty hours to seek God's help in a time of war. To this a Capuchin, Joseph von Ferno (known also to Thurston), added the practice of continuing the prayer throughout all the churches of Milan. Thurston was right however in identifying its place of origin.[9]

This kind of work was very congenial to Thurston and he wrote a great number of articles in the Jesuit periodical *The Month* and in the old *Catholic Encyclopedia* (1907–) on popular devotions and on the authorship and history of certain well known prayers. He wrote on the devotion of the Stations of the Cross (known in England by the fifteenth century) and more dangerously on the Rosary. He held that St Dominic had nothing to do with it and this caused something of a rumpus, the Dominicans understandably objecting. Thurston held that the devotion was propagated by Alain des Roches, OP, in the fifteenth century. The saying of the beads, 150 Paternosters in the course of a day was a practice of the laybrothers of the Cistercian order in the twelfth century. In a posthumous book (edited by Paul Grosjean, SJ) *Familiar Devotions* (1953) he considers 'The Sign of the Cross' (first attestation, Tertullian), The 'The Our Father in English' ('which art in heaven' was in use *before* the Reformation and so was not 'Protestant'), the *Anima Christi* (fourteenth century, so not written by St Ignatius of Loyola), the *Veni Sancte Spiritus* (firmly attributed to Stephen Langton, Archbishop of Cantebury, died 1228) and the *Memorare*. This prayer which for long was attributed to St Bernard was propagated by a priest called Claude Bernard in the seventeenth century and it appears printed on his portraits of similar date as 'Oraison du R. P. Bernard' and so became attributed to him as author. But it was known already to St Francis de Sales and seems to date from the fifteenth century. What is certain is that it was not written by St Bernard (died 1153) as most people thought and may still think. There are one or two phrases in it which can be found in the sermons of the saint.

Other items on the book include the authorship and dating of the *Salve Regina*, the *Regina caeli* and how the Hail Mary came to be what it is today (a rather longer development than most people think). Finally, he examines the use of the *De profundis* (psalm 129) as a prayer for the dead and the origins of the short doxology, the *Gloria Patri* which takes him back to the *Didache*!

For all this Thurston got little thanks. People do not like being disturbed in their pious beliefs about certain prayers and devotions. If for instance St Bernard was not the author of the *Memorare* they are inclined to think that it has been devalued. They do not like to think that devout people in the Middle Ages said only the half of the Hail Mary and so on. Thurston thought that the truth was all important and that holiness was so sacred that it must be shorn of all that turned people from its substance to its fringes, as Fr C. C. Martindale, SJ, perceptibly wrote of him.

Two other books that could be said to be concerned with the liturgy or rather with ceremonial were *The Holy Year of Jubliee* (1900) and *The Coronation Ceremonial* (1902), which hardly concerns us here. He published a book on *The Stations of the Cross* (1904) but great quantities of work appeared in *The Month* and the old *Catholic Encyclopaedia*, as well as in other periodicals and many of them are still consulted by scholars today. He wrote extensively on paranormal psychological phenomena but these writings are not relevant to our theme. It is difficult to assess the effect of Thurston's many writings but I think, it can be said that his work on the saints and his book on *Lent and Holy Week* made a contribution to the liturgical movement. By his critical work he swept away a good deal of rubbish and this was enlightening to those who read him. Others have built on what he began.

Bibliography

There is a Memoir, *Father Thurston* (1952) by Joseph Crehan, SJ, and a good notice by Michael J. Walsh in the *Dictionnaire de Spiritualité*, Fasc. XV. 1991, s. v. *Thurston*, Herbert Henry Charles, 1856–1939, kindly communicated to me by Mr Walsh.

Notes

1. Leo XIII gave him a medal.

2. Who however also contributed to the Supplement.

3. See Nigel Abercrombie, *The Life and Work of Edmund Bishop* (London, 1959), p 282.

4. Abercrombie, op cit, p 101.

5. It went into two editions (the second revised by Fortescue himself) and had an eleventh impression in 1955 with a few updatings in a Note by the present writer and a second additional list of books also. There was a French translation, *La Messe*, 1920.

6. See my *Worship in a Hidden Church* (1988), pp 88, 89.

7. If it was a down-payment rather than an advance on royalties Burns and Oates must have made a pile out of it.

8. Her cultus was due to a pious parish priest near Naples.

9. For this information see Nathan Mitchell, *Cult and Controversy* (Pueblo, NY. 1982, p 312).

CHAPTER XIII

Giacomo Moglia
and the Beginnings of the Italian Liturgical Movement

The traveller in Italy in the decades before Vatican II could be forgiven for thinking that there was no liturgical movement there. The developing liturgical practices, various forms of active participation, in Belgium, Germany and France seemed to be unknown in Italy. Parish churches were often filled with clutter and if there was any singing it was truly awful. Nothing could equal the harshness of the ancient ladies' voices trying to sing a mangled plainsong. Or there were those pompous high Masses when everything seemed to be sung *fortissimo* from beginning to end. In the nineteenth century the situation was worse. In 1884 the Congregation of Rites issued a very fierce bann on all kinds of secular music such as theatrical pieces or anything reminiscent of them; it forbade dance music of any kind, such as polkas, mazurkas, minuets, rounds, *schottishe*, 'varsoviennes' (?), quadrilles, galops, counterdances, 'lithuaniennes' (?), erotic or comic songs, romances …'. Also forbidden were excessively noisy musical instruments such as tambourines (or little drums), big drums, cymbals, or even the harpsichord or piano, both regarded as frivolous and unduly secular.[1] This was the background of Pius X's *Motu proprio* on church music which he issued almost immediately after his election as pope in 1903. It contained the germinal statement that the active participation of the people in the holy mysteries (the Mass and the Prayer of the Church) was the source of the Christian spirit. It led to the propagation of the singing of plainsong, the 'Gregorian', in many parish churches throughout the world but it was sometimes forgotten that the point of the *Motu proprio* was not simply that plainsong should be sung but that the *people* should sing it and thereby take an active part in the celebration of the liturgy. An Italian historian could write that the statement about active participation never appeared in any subsequent statement of the same pope during the rest of his pontificate, even in those acts of his, like the reform of the Breviary and the restoration of the celebration of the 'green' Sundays throughout the year, that concerned the liturgy.

Yet there was a liturgical movement in Italy which is associated with the name of Giacomo Moglia to whom we shall return in a moment. Partly contemporary with Moglia was Bishop Bonomelli, described as a 'man of lively intelligence'. In 1902 he published a pastoral letter *Sentimentalismo e formalismo in Religione...*' in which he stated that there was a need 'to prune the luxuriant growth of devotional practices' and to lead the people to the central truths of the faith. He followed this up with a more specific charge. In 1905 he issued another pastoral letter *Il Culto religioso: diffetti, abusi* in which he criticised the unbalanced devotion to the Sacred Heart of Jesus, which was a very unpopular thing to do. But in this letter he breathed not a word about the liturgy nor did he make mention of the *Motu proprio*. His thought seems to have been developing as in 1913 he wrote another pastoral on the Church (*La Chiesa*) in which he strongly expressed his desire that the people should study and understand the significance of the rites and prayers of the liturgy. If they did, they would not be praying simply as individuals but would get used to participating in it and would enter into its spirit. He wanted booklets with texts of the Mass and Vespers, with explanations, to be put in the hands of the people 'as in Switzerland, Germany, Holland and elsewhere'. He was evidently well informed. However he was opposed to translating the liturgy into the vernacular. In another work on the *Instruction of the Young in Christian Doctrine* he saw the liturgy simply as a means to nourish the devotion of the young but by 1912, two years before his death, he was becoming aware of the cautious liturgical movement in Genoa and when urged to bring out a revised edition of his *Instruction* he replied 'If I were to do what I would like to do and ought to do, I would be a Modernist and then the heavens would open'! E. Cattaneo who records the saying, remarks, 'Considering current opinion, he was certainly right'.[2]

Things were moving however and in the year that Bonomelli died Bishop Matteo Filipello wrote a pastoral letter with the title *La Liturgia parrochiale* which struck a new note, suggesting a pastoral liturgy, but this was not surprising as its ultimate origin was the Belgian liturgical movement emanating from Maredsous and Mont-César. In this letter and in clear terms he sketches out a basic theology of the Church with which to underpin the liturgy: Christians are of course part of the Church and if they are to be good Christians they should live the life of the Church. But 'the Church is a great family ... and you are members of this fami- ly.... The life of the Church is expressed in a special way in acts of worship, i.e. the liturgy.... These acts are not solitary and private, performed only by priests; they are official and public. That is, they are acts accomplished by the Church, by the people and in the name of the people. The Church wants them to be present not only bodily but with voice, mind, heart and soul.'

The liturgical movement as such can be said to have begun in Italy in 1930 and its initiator was Giacomo Moglia, a dynamic priest of the archdiocese of Genoa. He was born near Genoa in 1881 in the same town as Giacomo Lercaro. His family were in easy circumstances and he received the usual education of a middle class youth of the time. After studies in the *liceo* (*lycée*) in Genoa he entered the seminary there for his four years of theology. After ordination he graduated in that subject and being bright, indeed very intelligent, he was appointed as lecturer in Church History in the seminary and in due course he taught moral theology and liturgy. The rector was already enthusiastic about the liturgy and evidently communicated his enthusiasm to the young lecturer. Moglia who is described as lively, enterprising and a leader, was also what we would call a first class communi- cator. Whatever he taught was taken in by his students, he was by all accounts a fascinating speaker whether in the pulpit, in the lecture hall or in conversation. People, especially the young flocked to him. He was soon employed in the local curia and was made Canon Theologian.

But in these years before 1914 he was living in difficult and even dangerous times. The Modernist crisis was at its height, professors of theology were closely scrutinised and, for what was regarded as the slightest deviation from orthodoxy, they could be sacked. Moglia's biographer says that the mood of the time acted as a brake on any new projects and for the clergy it became a justifi- cation for doing nothing. The same writer says cryptically that Moglia was at one time suspected and suffered but survived. This is probably why he wrote nothing except the texts of the few homilies and talks. He was *'allergico della penna'*![3]

He probably made himself unpopular by expressing his views
on the deplorable habits of some of the clergy. He stigmatised
one of them who read banns of marriage and other announce-
ments during the Canon of the Mass, stopping only for the consecration and continuing afterwards. Likewise, he objected to
the custom, very widespread in Italy, of reciting the rosary
aloud during Mass. Speaking to priests on one occasion he said
'Act – celebrate – as if you believed in what you are doing, since
you look as if you don't.' These and other criticisms can hardly
have endeared him to the authorities in Rome. Even in Genoa
the mood and the general atmosphere was not propitious for the
kind of liturgical movement that Moglia initiated. Writing in his
memoir of Moglia, Cardinal Lercaro said that the Genoese were
strongly attached 'to the customs, of a rich, showy and baroque
tradition' of liturgy.[4]

Nonetheless he persevered and given his personality it is not
surprising that he attracted the young and among them he began.
He did what he could to initiate them into active participation,
as he did when he was made chaplain to an institute for young
trainee-workers, and when army chaplain he brought out a
booklet to guide the soldiers towards active participation. On
account of the economic difficulties of the time it had to cease
publication. Later, and also for the young, he translated and
edited another booklet containing Prime and Compline and the
daily missal of Dom Lefevbre. After 1930 he arranged the publication in Latin and Italian of Mass leaflets to assist participation.
This was later taken up by the *Opera della Regalità* which was
under the aegis of Dr A. Gemelli, the rector of the Catholic
University of Milan.

In these efforts we can see the influence of the Belgian movement which was the first to provide bi-lingual Mass leaflets that
were distributed free outside churches as the people went in.

In 1930 Moglia founded the *Apostolato Liturgico* which, it is interesting to note, was not a purely clerical organisation. There were
three sections (*rami*), one for the clergy, one for youths and one
for girls. The organisation prepared and offered courses in the
study of the Bible, in theology, liturgy, and Christian doctrine.
There were also courses to help in the preparation for First
Communion and for confirmation. At the time these last two

courses were of particular importance. Mussolini, then at the height of his power, had 'organised' the youth of the country into the Ballila and the whole question of Christian education in the schools was under threat. In addition, other 'aids' were published for the celebration of other sacraments, for the Mass and for Vespers.

In all this work he was supported by Giacomo Lercaro, later Cardinal Archbishop of Bologna and President after the Council of the Consilium/Congregation for Worship, by Emilio Guano who also became a bishop, and by Giuseppe Siri who became Cardinal Archbishop of Genoa. A priest called Giuseppe Cavalleri succeeded Mgr Moglia after his early death at the age of sixty in 1941.

Moglia, then, did not work alone, it was not his way, and if it be asked what was the result of his apostolate one or two factors have to be taken into account. As in other countries, in Belgium where the liturgical movement had its origin, in Germany where so much was done at a liturgico-theological level (Maria-Laach) and in France where the liturgical movement was flourishing but only in certain sectors (the Young Christian Workers, the Y.C. Students etc.), the liturgical movement in Italy made its way only slowly. Italians were very traditional in their ways, they were greatly given to individualistic devotions and they had a weak sense of community; low Masses in side-chapels were what they preferred. Secondly, the dominance of Mussolini and his Fascist government did not make life for the Church easy, and, finally, Italy had a quite appalling time in the Second World War when it became the battlefield for two forces, the Allies and the Hitlerite Germans who between them wrought great damage and caused great loss of life.[5] All had to begin all over again after the war and it was in the 1950s and 1960s that men like Lercaro and Bugnini made their great contribution to the reform of the liturgy.

Not only did Moglia not work alone but there were others giving impetus to new thinking and action. The Benedictine contribution came from North West Italy (and indeed beyond) with the foundation of the monastery of Finalpia which issued the first number of the *Rivista Liturgica* in 1914 in which the editor, Dom Emanuele Caronti, stated its aims. His intent was to high-light the principal aspects of the liturgy. He wanted to present the liturgy as something to be loved and practised as the religious life that belongs to every Christian because it is the life of the Church. Piety should be fashioned by a Catholic sense, i.e. with the sense of Christ himself. One is reminded of Dom Lambert Beauduin's *Piété de l'Englise* (1914) of which one finds echoes in much of the Italian writings about liturgy at this time or a little later. From Subiaco came a *Liturgical Manual for the use of those who attend Benedictine churches*. Among the names associated with the liturgical effort one notes that of Adriano Bernareggi, Bishop of Bergamo, who was the bishop of Angelo Roncalli, later Pope John XXIII.[6] There was also the name of Mario Righetti, monk of Finalpia who devoted himself to scholarship and produced the four-volume *Storia Liturgica* (2nd ed 1950–) in which he covered not only the history of the Mass but that of the sacraments, the Divine Office and the Liturgical Year. Other names could be mentioned but it was not until after the Second Vatican Council that the bishops of Italy took up the promotion of the liturgy and this they have done with great vigour and intelligence.

Bibliography

Information about Mgr Moglia is derived from *Liturgia, Ieri, Oggi, Sempre*. Atti del Convegno... 30 September - 2 October, 1991, in celebration of the 50th Anniversary of the death of Giacomo Moglia. Edited by the Figlie della Carità, a congregation of religious sisters founded by him to assist him in his work and to continue it after him. This they have done. There are three presentations of him and his life, rather rhetorical in style. The account given above depends on the first: *Mons. Moglia Maestro e Antesignano per l'Oggi e per il Domani*, pp 89–100.

Notes

1. See O. Rousseau, *Histoire du Movement Liturgique* (Paris, 1945), p 155. There seems to be a case for a similar bann nowadays!

2. For the above quotation see E. Cattaneo, *Il Culto Cristiano in Occidente*, pp 589–592.

3. See Alessandro Piazza in *Liturgia, Ieri, Oggi, Sempre* (Genova, 1992), pp 90, 91.

4. Quoted in the above article, p 93.

5. There are historians who say that the Italian war was an unnecessary war.

6. For the above see E. Cattaneo, *Il Culto...*, p 596.

CHAPTER XIV

The Question of Language:
Saints Cyril and Methodius

There are two questions about language. First, how do we talk about God? A difficult matter, because human language can never encapsulate the mystery of God which goes beyond all our powers of expression. Is God male or female? St Thomas said that God is beyond genus and therefore is neither male nor female but beyond both. All words then about God are analogous: both true and only partly true, like what we know in this sublunary order and unlike it. The Bible and the liturgy, taking its vocabulary from it, uses a great number of images and metaphors in an endeavour to say something true about God, and we can be grateful that they do for otherwise we should be dumb. Yet images and metaphors grow stale or misleading and the Christian community has to make efforts all the time to find ways of talking about God that are acceptable and comprehensible to the people of this age or of any to come. This will eventually affect the liturgy, the way we pray, though we shall throw away the biblical data at our peril.

It is not however this sort of question that I wish to broach here. By language I mean the languages that people speak and have spoken throughout time, so many and so various that they cannot be counted. And what language has been used in worship has in the West always been something of a problem. The continued use of Latin when it had ceased to be the language of the people reduced their participation in the liturgy and provided a problem of its own. From the time of the Council of Trent when modern languages had become mature, with noble literatures, there were queries about the use of Latin in our worship. It was not, and is not, a new question, as so many seem to have thought; it is a very old question which was faced and solved in the early centuries of the Church.

The Last Supper was celebrated in Aramaic, the language of the people of Palestine at the time, but when the Church moved out into the Gentile Greek-speaking world the language of the eucharist became Greek. All the accounts of the institution of the eucharist, those in I Corinthians, in Mark, Matthew and Luke are in Greek. The lingua franca, the *koiné* as it was called, of the Greco-Roman Empire was Greek and there was what seems to have been a large colony of Greek-speaking Jews in Rome (cf Acts 28:23–25; Rom 16:3–15). To them St Paul wrote his letter in Greek. If we look outside Rome to southern Gaul we find that the Church at Lyons was Greek-speaking. Founded as it seems early in the second century, its famous bishop, Irenaeus wrote in Greek. There was also a Greek-speaking colony in Marseilles (Massilia) and no doubt elsewhere along the Mediterranean seaboard. Only North Africa and Spain, it seems, were Latin zones though Tertullian knew Greek well but wrote in Latin, except for one of his works.

It was however in North Africa that a change was first made. The first translation of the Bible (from the Greek Septuagint) was made there and since, as in countries in the Middle East the Bible was translated into the local languages so that it could be used in the liturgy, it may well have been done in Africa for the same reason, though unfortunately we have no liturgical texts of the second century.[1] Manuscripts of the translation of the Bible were copied (in great numbers, as St Jerome observed) and circulated in Italy (hence the term *Itala*) or were made there. Already then, and even in the West, the principal was established that the liturgy should be in the language of the people. As we know from the descriptions of the eucharist by St Justin the Martyr who was working in Rome about 150 the language of the rite was Greek.

When then did the Church of Rome change from Greek to Latin? Much has been written about this matter and all is not clear. It seems however that Latin was losing ground in third century Rome. There were both Greek and Latin speaking Christians and the Old Roman Creed (the parent of the Apostles' Creed) existed in Greek and Latin. It was of course a liturgical text used in baptism. There are writings in Latin, such as Novatian's on the Trinity, in which there are overtones of what might well have been liturgical Latin. He died in the persecution of Valerian in 250. Popes regularly corresponded in Latin with bishops in

North Africa and it is in the writings from that country, those of
Tertullian (mentioned above) and St Cyprian (+258) especially,
that we find what are undoubtedly liturgical phrases. Thus, in
the latter's commentary on the Lord's Prayer (*De Oratione
Dominica*, c 31) there are the phrases that to this day introduce
the eucharistic prayer: *Sursum corda. Habemus ad Dominum.* ('Lift
up your hearts…') and perhaps the origin of the invitatory to the
Lord's Prayer as it is recited in the eucharist: *salutaria monita et
praecepta divina* (*Praeceptis salutaribus moniti* … in the Roman
Missal). There are also phrases that suggest they were influenced by or were 'borrowed' from the liturgy by the author
(whoever he was) of the *Te Deum*. Not only then was the language of the Latin liturgy being forged, it had already reached an
advanced stage of maturity. It is certain that well before the end
of the fourth century Latin had already established itself as a liturgical language. This is very apparent for Rome from the homilies
of Pope St Leo the Great (+461) who seems at times to be quoting
pre-existing liturgical phrases (*Dignum et iustum est*) and collects
but also, as is most probable, wrote them himself. The collect for
the Third Mass, Christmas Day, is found in so many words in
one of his Christian homilies. Even more important the central
part of the Roman Canon appears in Latin in the *De Sacramentis*
(IV, 21–22) of St Ambrose (+397). It evidently existed before
since he quotes it. Other fragments of the Canon also exist and
they *may* be of the same date.

Between, then, 250 and 350 the liturgy of Rome and Italy had become a Latin liturgy. The change evidently met the needs of the
people and seems to have been made without protest. It was in
this way that the liturgical language of the West became Latin,
not only in Rome but in the great metropolitan centres like
Milan and Lyons and the whole region of southern Gaul where
the Gallican rite flourished. As far as we know the Spanish (or
Mozarabic) rite was always in Latin and with some echoes of the
Roman rite but in the course of time both the Spanish and the
Gallican liturgies were influenced by the eastern churches. The
Filioque clause in the Creed came via the Spanish church and in
Latin.

During the centuries that followed Latin remained a living language at least in Italy and no doubt in Spain but the barbarian
invasions eventually brought into the church peoples without any

Latin culture and whose languages had not reached any literary maturity. It would not have been possible, even if there had been any desire for it on the part of the clergy, to translate the liturgy into innumerable dialects. This was the situation in the eighth century when Charlemagne introduced the Roman liturgy in the lands he had conquered, in what we now call Germany, France and indeed elsewhere. The Roman liturgy, somewhat adapted to the needs of the world north of the Alps, now became the official liturgy.

But if the language of the liturgy perforce remained in Latin, the Carolingian church, actively spurred on by Charlemagne and his son Louis and their successors, made strenuous efforts to instruct the new Christians and the bulk of this instruction was centred upon the liturgy. Certain prayers, for example the Lord's Prayer and the Creed, must be taught to the people since they had to recite the Creed in baptism and the Lord's Prayer was sung at Mass. The people should understand it. As the English monk Alcuin wrote to a friend, it is not much use forcing people to be baptised and to pay the tithe (!) if they do not understand what they are doing. Priests, whose education was vigorously taken in hand, were urged to preach to the people in their own tongue, 'that is in the vernacular dialects of the particular regions served by the diocese'. Texts of various sorts survive in primitive German that show that priests did preach in the vernacular and that there were prayers like the Lord's Prayer and the Creed in the vernacular. A Council of Tours in 813 ordered that sermons on the basic principles of Christian living should be translated into popular Latin ('rusticam romanam linguam', presumably the slowly developing 'French' language) and into German so that all may the more easily understand what is said. For England the homilies of Aelfric in Anglo-Saxon survive to this day. These and other homilies were usually based on the liturgical year.

It seems to have been assumed that the people, perhaps through this constant preaching and instruction, would have some idea of the meaning of some of the Latin texts with their chants for in his Capitularies Charlemagne urges that the people should sing the Sanctus and perhaps other chants. In addition to the education of the clergy which was strongly pressed by council and synod, schools for boys were set up so that they could learn Latin as well as plainsong. It is of course difficult if not impossible to assess the effect of this unceasing campaign but it shows that the Carolingians, often much criticised for dragooning people into the Church, were concerned that, once in, they should have some grasp of their new faith and some understanding of the liturgy. It is possible that these new Christians were better instructed than their posterity of later centuries when, because Christendom was Catholic, it was thought that instruction was of less importance.[2]

The Eastern Churches differed from Rome in their policy of language. There were liturgies in Greek (Antioch, Constantinople, Alexandia (also Greek), Syriac (East and West) and, later in Egypt, Coptic which is the original Egyptian language put into Greek letters. But also in existence were languages like Armenian and Georgian (south Russia) from an early age. Other languages were and are still in use with an extensive use of Arabic where it has become the usually spoken language. The general principle of the Eastern Churches is that the liturgy should be celebrated in the language of the people. Thus the numerous Russian Orthodox Church took its liturgy (and its faith) from Constantinople but turned its liturgical language into Old Russian (*staroslav*).

Latin was destined to be the language of the Roman and other rites of the West but before this was completely achieved there was a contest and indeed conflict in the border lands between the East and the West. Moravia (now part of the Czech Republic) was on the way to becoming Christian under German influence but the German missionaries insisted on Latin and could not preach or instruct in the local language. The people were much put off by this. Constantinople regarded this area as well as Bulgaria as in its sphere of influence, both political and ecclesiastical. News came of events in Moravia and eventually two brothers, one Constantine (later Cyril) and Methodius were sent to the region. Both were learned and, as we can see now, openminded. If the Moravians were to be converted and if they were to be able to worship with understanding, it would be necessary to evangelise them in their own language and to worship in it. Cyril then set to work and produce a liturgy and translations of parts of the Bible in Glagolitic thus giving the people a literary language for the first time. This brought success for Cyril and Methodius, the people accepted their teaching and their liturgy.

News of this mission reached Rome about 867 and the two brothers were invited to Rome. As a gift they brought the alleged relics of St Clement of Rome which greatly pleased the pope, Hadrian II, and the Roman officials. The pope had the liturgical books examined and 'approved of the brave and intelligent innovations of the two missionaries'. Unhappily Cyril died in Rome where he was given a splendid funeral (869). Methodius was consecrated archbishop and appointed to the ancient see of Sirmium (Mitrovitza) in Pannonia (Yugoslavia) and the regions to the North and the East, including of course Moravia. He was not able to take up his office or his duties.

It was a turbulent time and there was a fierce struggle between the Moravians and the Germans. Into the details of it we cannot go here. To be brief, Methodius was imprisoned for two years in a tower in Bavaria where he suffered greatly. A new pope John VIII heard of this, he strongly condemned the Germans and Methodius was released. His mission was inhibited by the ruler of Moravia who was a turn-coat, accusations about his orthodoxy were made and the pope called him to Rome. Methodius completely justified himself, his orthodoxy and his use of a liturgical language understood by the people. The pope was satisfied and sent Methodius back with a strong letter confirming him as archbishop and the use of Glagolitic. Incredibly however the pope also appointed a German, Wiching, as a suffragan to Methodius and he proved to be Methodius's worst enemy. Falsifying the papal letter (of which he had obtained a copy) he proclaimed that Methodius had not received any 'concessions' and that he had sworn on the Tomb of the Apostle in Rome *not* to use the language of the Slavs in liturgy or preaching. When the pope heard of this he repudiated the faked letter and stated that Methodius was right and that he, the pope, had not changed his views.

It is not surprising that eventually Methodius went back to Constantinople, perhaps for consolation, but also to continue his work of translating the Bible. He died full of honour in 884.

After his death Wiching managed to persuade a new pope to reject Methodius's work and Wiching carried out a persecution of his followers. Gorazd whom Methodius had appointed as his successor had to flee and other followers trickled into Bulgaria where the Cyrillic alphabet was born.

All seemed lost but not entirely. The Glagolitic liturgy survived in regions of Croatia and Dalmatia. Its history is however very complicated. The letter of John VIII was deciphered and partly reconstructed by monks of Monte Cassino in the eleventh century and about 1265 it was restored to the papal archives. Without knowing this, Innocent IV gave the first permission to use a Slav liturgy in 1248, and later in 1346 when the letter of John VIII was known, Clement VI gave a second permission. As late as the seventeenth century popes Urban VIII and Innocent X gave a further permission. Thus, as C. Korolevskij remarks, the principle formulated by John VIII, was revived: 'The practice of singing the Mass in the Slav language or the reading of the holy Gospel or the divine lessons of the Old and the New Testament has nothing against sound faith or doctrine if they are well translated and explained. The same applies to the singing of the hours of the Office.'3

The Slavonic liturgy went on existing and being celebrated in a Benedictine monastery called Emmaus near Prague in the fourteenth century, it ceased with the troubles associated with Jan Huss in the fifteenth century, was restored at the end of the sixteenth century and came to an end in that place only when the community died out in 1635 and the monastery was peopled by Spanish monks from Montserrat. Nonetheless under Pope Innocent X the liturgical books underwent revision, and were approved by him, the Glagolitic being the language they contained. There were further editions, one in the eighteenth century, but the most important was the revision in the pontificate of Pius XI in 1927, a revised edition printed and published by the Vatican Press. There was also a Ritual for the administration of the sacraments dated 1887 and a later book in the dialect of Dalmatia that appeared with papal approval in 1932/3. In it were to be found the epistles and gospels for Sundays and feast days, sequences and certain liturgical rites like that of Candlemas and Ash Wednesday. Finally, not to give all the details of the various books and their editions, in the Concordat with the then Yugoslavia in 1935 the Holy See confirmed the use of Slavonic in the liturgy with the forms ratified by Leo XIII and Pius X. The document stated that the bishops might allow the use of Slavonic in parishes where it was the unanimous wish of the people. The point about the wish of the people is very important; if they wanted Slavonic they could have it.4

Other instances of translations of the Roman rite can be found. The Dominican liturgical books were translated into Greek for use in and near Constantinople and further afield into Armenian. It may be thought that these permissions were given in view of special needs and occasions, yet they are breaches of what most people before Vatican II regarded as an unbreakable law. There never was a law; there was custom and what was too little known is that the Council of Trent, which some like to quote in this context, said that it was not expedient (*non expedit*) to use vernacular languages at the time. Latin, the classical Latin of the Renaissance had tremendous prestige, the Fathers of the Council had been brought up on it, and in their view the vernaculars of their time were still fluid. That was of course partly true though they would have known nothing of Ronsard's poems in France or of the Book of Common Prayer and Shakespeare in England. What troubled them most was that the Reformers had made of the vernacular a theological principle. All had to hear the word of God to be saved, faith came by hearing, and if the people could not hear the church services in their own language they were useless. Yet there were some at the Council of Trent who were aware of the difficulties raised by a Latin liturgy. The only English bishop at the Council of Trent, Thomas Goldwell, Bishop of St Asaph, pleaded for some English in the liturgy and, if that were not possible, that the rites of the liturgy should be explained to the people. He may have been thinking of the efforts made by Cardinal Pole and Bishop Bonner in the restored church under Mary Tudor to instruct the people about the Mass and other parts of the liturgy.[5] The Council contented itself with saying that the Mass contains much for the instruction of the people, that pastors of souls should often explain what is read and done, not only the epistle and the gospel but the ceremonies and their meaning, and this *inter Missarum sollemnia*, during the course of the celebration.[6] This left open the possibility of commentaries of one sort or another during the Mass but it was not until the last phase of the liturgical movement, from about 1945 onwards, that many realised that this was a possibility and made use of it. Even so, it did not prove very satisfactory, commentaries could detract from attention to the Mass as did the 'voice-over' when that was used for the Latin texts said in a low voice.

The decision of the Council of Trent was understandable at the time but the general stance of the Church hardened afterwards. There developed the siege mentality. Even a powerful church like that of France seemed almost obsessed by the threat of Protestantism. Then there were the Jansenists and Jansenisers who seemed to be agitating for a vernacular liturgy (though in fact they were not; they wanted better participation). The Church in the nineteenth century felt itself to be under attack from a hostile and ever more secularised world and was afraid to change anything. It was not until this century that the clergy and the laity were convinced that the gap between a largely not understood liturgy and a true participation in it could only be closed by a reform of the liturgy and the use of the people's languages in its celebration. It was the achievement of the Second Vatican Council to have done this. If there is regret that the use of Latin has largely disappeared from our liturgy it must be seen as offering a large and necessary compensation; people, anyone, can now approach God through a liturgy that speaks directly to them and which they can pray in their own language. Perhaps not all is well but the reasons for that have nothing to do with the vernacular as such. If our worship at times and in some places has become dull, if it has become trivialised by poor music and rubbishy, self-regarding 'songs', that is because too many have lost a sense of the wonder and mystery of God and because we are living in a declining culture.

Notes

1. There are descriptions of liturgical services in various works of Tertullian (e.g. *De Baptismo*) and they were celebrated in Latin, the language of the people.

2. For the information about the Carolingian church see Rosamund McKitterick, *The Frankish Church and the Carolingian Reforms*, 789–895 (London, Royal Historical Society, 1977), from which quotations in the previous two paragraphs are taken.

3. C. Korolevskij, *Liturgie en Langue Vivante*, (Paris, 1955), p 128, with reference to Migne, Pat. Lat. t. 126, c. 906.

4. For all the foregoing see Korolevskij, op cit, pp 114–135. For the history of the times and troubles of St Cyril and St Methodius see E. Amann, *L'Époque Carolingienne*, Paris, 1947 (*Hist de l'Église*, Fliche et Martin, 6), pp 454–501.

5. See Eamon Duffy, *The Stripping of the Altars* (Yale Press Newhaven, London, 1992), pp 529, 533.

6. See A. G. Martimort, *La Maison-Dieu*, 11, 1947, 'La discipline de l'Église en matière de langue liturgique', pp 40–45.

I have not thought to include an account of the 'Chinese Rites' and of Fr Matteo Ricci's attempt at the inculturation of the Roman liturgy in China. It is a vast and contentious subject. Suffice it to say that the *Roman Missal* and other liturgical books were translated into Chinese (mandarin) in 1670 and used until suppressed in 1680 (See C. Korolevskij, *Liturgie en Langue Vivante*, p 151)

CHAPTER XV

Active Participation
and the Problem of Music

Throughout the recorded history of the liturgy in the West there has been a certain tension between music and liturgy, indeed almost a suspicion of it. We remember the scruple of St Augustine who was afraid of being almost seduced by it, led away from God, and wanted 'to banish all the melodies and sweet chants used for David's psalter' but he decided to follow the bishops, Athanasius in the East and Ambrose in the West. He recalled the days of his conversion and how he was moved not so much by the chants as by the words when they were sung 'with a clear voice and entirely appropriate modulation'.[1] For him the words were all-important. There has also been a tension between music and the worshipping community who are called upon to take part vocally in the celebration of the liturgy. Crudely, who should sing what and when? A glance into the past may help us to see what the problem was (and to some extent still is) and how a satisfactory situation came to be changed into an unsatisfactory one.

The term 'active participation' was unknown in the early centuries of the Church. It existed, it was taken for granted, the liturgy was the act of a community, no one thought of 'private celebrations'. All heard the word of God in their own language, all responded to 'Lift up your hearts' before the eucharistic prayer, all gave their assent to the eucharistic prayer with 'Amen' and, as St Ambrose tells us, all replied 'Amen' to the words of the celebrant when he said to them 'The body of Christ, the blood of Christ' at holy communion. As we read in Augustine's *Commentaries on the Psalms*, all sang the responses to the psalms as they were sung at the eucharist. From a later writer Cassiodorus (+570) we learn that the Alleluias that followed the responsorial psalm were sung by the people: 'This (the Alleluia) is peculiar to the churches of God and is especially appropriate to the holy festivals. The tongue of the singer rejoices in it; *joyfully the community repeat it*; and like something good of which we cannot have enough, it is renewed in ever varying neums'. If the 'neums' were varied they were evidently not too elaborate for the people to sing. In Rome in the time of St Gregory the Great it could be said that 'Running through the Mass was a continual dialogue between the celebrant and the assembled faithful, whose response formed a striking element in the corporate celebration'.[2]

Gradually however chants that had been sung by the people were taken over first by the clergy and then by the choir (*schola*). Between the latter part of the seventh century and the ninth the Kyrie (originally a simple response to a litany) and then the Gloria (when sung) ended up by being sung by the specialists. The Sanctus which was introduced into the Mass of the Roman rite in the early fifth century had always been a congregational chant sung by the celebrant and the people together. This too was absorbed by the *schola*. The Agnus Dei, also part of a litany, was introduced into the rite by Pope Sergius I (+701) to accompany the breaking of the bread (a long and complicated process in the papal rite) and was at first sung by the clergy and the people, but eventually it suffered the same fate as the rest of the ordinary of the Mass.[3] Another chant that was once the song of the people was not only taken over by the *schola* but was reduced to single verse. From the earliest days psalm 33 (34) on account of the words 'Taste and see that the Lord is good' had been sung by the people (no doubt responsorially) as they went to receive holy communion.

As is well known the Creed was not introduced into the Mass in Rome until 1014 – at the instance of the German Emperor! It had however been sung in the Frankish empire since the ninth century and was sung by the people with the clergy at that time. In Rome however it was not sung by the people though Credo I is a syllabic chant which one supposes they could have managed. Credo III which in the years before Vatican II was sung with gusto by the people (and still is in a few places) was a late composition of the sixteenth or even seventeenth century.

All this development, if such it can be called, came from the elaboration of music. The graduals for instance which replaced the responsorial psalm (from which they derived) became so difficult and complicated that they could only be sung by experts (for the most part monks) and not only were these texts very long, but the elaboration of the chant was such as to obscure rather than communicate the words. The same can be said of introits, offertoria and responsories of various kinds. In the tension between music and word as well as the people's participation, word and people lost. Plainsong which in this century has been used as a means to promote active participation had become elaborate even for those texts, Kyrie and the rest, which the people were invited to sing. It could be said that there was a certain success but all the same it was a tour de force to sing them well and often enough they were sung badly.

There was however worse to come. In the thirteenth century a form of polyphony developed that has been called 'heterophony' which 'super-imposed different syllables, words or even texts' on a certain base so that the voices were singing different melodies, some in the vernacular, so that it was impossible to distinguish the words that were supposed to be sung.[4] This was condemned by Pope John XXII in 1324–5 as music 'that intoxicates the ears and benumbs the souls of the singers'; the primacy of the liturgical act must be preserved 'to keep the soul of each one awake without the words suffering.[5] Another undesirable practice in the Middle Ages was the 'stuffing' (farcing) of the liturgical texts with phrases that were actually sung. Examples of this can be found in the *Kyriale* (Kyrie XI, *Orbis factor*) which could prolong and complicate the authentic text. Even later, when church music was supposed to have been cleaned up, composers borrowed musical themes from well known and not very appropriate songs such as *L'homme armé* and *Bayse-moi, ma mie* (Kiss me, my love).[6]

These and other abuses in the celebration of the liturgy attracted the attention of the fathers of the Council of Trent. They appointed a commission which drew up a list of some seventy-nine abuses, most of them concerning the Mass. We read of 'superstitious' Masses, those celebrated with more candles than another and thought to be more 'efficacious', those celebrated under the invocation of a sometimes obscure saint were favoured by others for the same reason. The fathers, realising that a council cannot reform a liturgy, committed the whole matter to the pope and in due course came the Breviary of 1568 and the Missal of 1570. But they did pronounce on church music. They condemned 'That type of music in which there is anything lascivious or impure, whether by the playing of the organ or by singing, is to be excluded from the churches... in order that the house of God may be said to be, and may actually be, a house of prayer'.[7] They did not condemn polyphony but it is said that in response to another commission in Rome Palestrina saved it.

When we move into the great age of polyphony (Palestrina, Victoria, Byrd and O. de Lassus) we are aware that this is religious music which by its very excellence draws the human mind and soul Godward. But one needs to have considerable musical expertise to appreciate it and even more skill to turn it into personal prayer. And however good it may be as music, it is usually very difficult to distinguish the words unless one has a text before one or it is very familiar. In any case by reason of its difficulty it is beyond the capability of almost all parish choirs. It has to be said also that it was composed for the Mass as it was and not as it is now. The nature of the *Kyrie* as the response to a series of invocations is completely lost, the Sanctus is too long, overlapping and overshadowing the eucharistic prayer and the Agnus Dei is similarly too long. 'Propers' like introits and graduals seem to have been neglected and plainsong was anyway in decline. With the coming of the Baroque Masses (and settings of Vespers) the situation got worse. These Masses had little regard for the structure of the Mass or the nature of the verbal texts which they accompanied – more or less. A Gloria for instance could take twenty minutes, and in spite of those who have maintained that one can participate by listening (as indeed one can in a normal liturgy) attention flags and one longs for the performance to be over. In the seventeenth century Pope Urban VIII felt it necessary to say that music is servant of the Mass not the Mass of the music. A true saying it has been necessary to repeat in more recent times. Pius X in his *Motu proprio* of 1903 pronounced as follows:

'In general it must be considered to be a very grave abuse when the liturgy in ecclesiastical functions is made to appear secondary to and in a manner at the service of the music, for music is merely a part of the liturgy and its humble handmaid'.

Has the battle for the priority of the word been won? Only

partly. You can still have a large assembly when classical settings are sung, when there is no participation of the people and even the responsorial psalm is taken over by the choir. You can have the first part of the Mass, the Liturgy of the Word, well celebrated *with* participation of the people, yet everything after that, except for the Sanctus and the Agnus Dei, is said. On such occasions the celebrant, whether bishop or priest, does not sing even the dialogue before the eucharistic prayer, much less the Preface or any part of the eucharistic prayer. Here word, at precisely the moment when the word needs enhancing, is bereft of the power it might have.

Two things, fundamental things, are lacking in such situations. The first is that even now the hierarchical nature of the liturgical assembly does not seem to be well understood. Let us consider this point first.

A custom seems to have grown whereby over and over again and in a vast number of places a sung Mass (not usually called such) is one that is accompanied by hymns, usually four (the 'Hymn–sandwich'). Thousands of parishes never *sing Mass*, that is they never sing those texts of the missal that in fact make up the rite of the Mass. A Sung Mass is one where celebrant and people sing those parts of the Mass that respectively belong to them. These are called the ministerial chants; first, those that the presider addresses to the people and to which they reply; and secondly, the chants which the people sing *with* the presider, the Gloria, the Sanctus etc.. The General Instruction attached to the Roman Missal of 1970 puts this matter quite strongly. Granting that not every text can be sung at every celebration, it yet emphasises the importance of the ministerial texts and then those sung by the people with the presider (sometimes called the 'common' texts): 'When deciding which parts of the Mass are actually to be sung, preference should be given to those which are more important, *especially those which the priest or one of his assistants is to sing in alternation with the people, or which he and they are to sing together*' (No 19). It is possible to sing the ministerial texts (those addressed by the presider to the people and their response) on almost every occasion. No choir is required, the plainsong settings in the missal are easy enough (though not always elegant) and can soon be learnt. In this way a Mass can be honestly and truly sung, the word of the rite has its proper place

and prominence and is borne along by a simple chant that rein-
forces its meaning.

In considering the first point about the distribution of roles in
the celebration, there is much that could be said about the importance and competence of readers. They are ministers of the
word, God's word, and if they are to fulfil their role they need
not only training in reading but education in the scriptures. It is
not possible to read intelligently and with conviction what you
do not understand. But that is a big question and I will restrict
my remarks to the choir and the nature of liturgical music.

Just as the choir is at the service of the assembly, helping it to
sing and so pray well, so is music. It is at the service of the word,
it is functional. It is sometimes thought that this is to degrade it.
But all the arts used in the liturgy are its servants, whether
sculpture, pictures or architecture itself. They are conditioned
by the purpose for which they are made and they receive their
dignity, their high dignity, from the liturgy itself. The iconographers
of the Byzantine rite, working within very definite rules, made
icons that are the admiration of the very secular world of today.
The anonymous 'architect' or the humble craftsman of the Middle
Ages who carved choir stalls, both working within a tradition
that at once imposed restraints and gave purpose, were servants
whose work is still admired. The same is true of music. It par-
takes of the total 'sacramentality' of the liturgy which is most
clearly seen in the *words* of institution (especially when they are
sung). Music then as it were becomes con-corporate with the
word that in the eucharistic prayer becomes the Word of God.
As the Constitution on the Liturgy, repeating the *Motu proprio* of
Pius X, states, music when wedded to the words is an integral
part of the liturgy, forming part of the liturgy in a way that no
other art does or can.

The same text, again repeating Pius X, states that 'the more intimately church music is linked with the liturgical action the holier
it will be' and in saying that it is 'holy' both the Constitution and
the pope were thinking primarily of plainsong and secondly of
classical polyphony which was undergoing a revival at the
beginning of this century. Neither could have realised what
would happen after the liturgy had been turned into the many
languages of the many peoples of the world. This has brought

new problems and rather different ones from those that existed
in the past. There is no doubt that the people participate vocally
but practice and the quality of the means are at times questionable. There are certain 'popular' Masses, sometimes the so-
called Children's Masses (i.e. correctly, Masses with Children)
when the responsorial psalm is either omitted or replaced by
something that may be a remote paraphrase (with no relevance
to the scriptures of the day) and it may be sung through in such
a way that the adults present cannot respond. Sometimes, even
now, choirs take over chants that belong to the people and do
not seem to realise that their role is to support the people and help
them to sing well what might otherwise be difficult to sing
without their support. It is one of the unhappier results of the
liturgical reform that the notion got about that choirs were unnecessary. Some were even dismissed (perhaps they were ir-
reformable!). It does not seem to be understood even now that
good congregational singing needs the support of a properly informed and well trained choir.

The lack of quality of so much of the music now sung is another
cause for concern. It is not just a question of good taste. A deep
and important principle is at stake. As the Constitution on the
Liturgy states, the end-purpose of liturgical music is first the
glory of God and secondly the sanctification of the faithful.
Music that does not lead to the glory and praise of God lacks an
essential quality of liturgical music for the whole purpose of the
liturgy is to draw people to God, to enter into union with him
and to open themselves out to him so that they can receive his
love, his grace and his blessings. Yet much that is sung in our
churches nowadays seems to be self-regarding both in words
and music. The words are often trivial and the music more or
less imitates what is heard in the 'profane' world. The notion got
about in the 1970s that the young would be attracted by that sort
of music. They could come and strum (inexpertly) their guitars,
electronically amplified, and beat their drums and wave their
tambourines. It attracted some for a time and if the 'programme'
continued, the same songs were repeated again and again until
they and everyone else got bored. In all this the people involved
were not really *singing* the Mass. They were singing something
parallel to it so that one could not say this was genuine participation. Of course verbal responses were made such as 'And also
with you' but the texts of the Mass were not sung nor responded

to with song. Perhaps all this is now on the wane if only because the young have disappeared and that is very sad.

It would seem to be time that pastors and musicians should reconsider the qualities required of liturgical music as laid down by Pius X and the Second Vatican Council in the Constitution on the Liturgy (Nos 112-121). The first quality is 'holiness' which may seem an odd word to attach to music, which is morally neutral. But it has two aspects, one negative and one positive. Negatively, the Church rejects what is 'worldly' and profane, as it has done through the centuries – and we seem to have suffered an invasion of the profane in recent years. Positively, 'music acquires this objective sanctity by becoming integrated into the sacred action, and in proportion to its integration'.[8] Or, as the Constitution puts it, 'Sacred music is to be considered the more holy in proportion as it is more closely connected with the liturgical action'. Perhaps it is significant that in more recent years the Taizé chants which have become popular in many places are the fruit of a contemplative community who are keenly aware of the presence of God among them and the vast assemblies whom they serve. The music is integral to their liturgies. Gelineau speaks of music being consecrated by its use in the liturgy and because of this 'the manner in which the music is performed should likewise *participate in the respect and hieratic character of the ritual action'*. This may seem over solemn, even too straight-laced, but different rites and different celebrations can range from exultant praise and thanksgiving to supplication for the needs of human beings. The *nature* of the celebration must be respected.

Closely connected with this is that liturgical music must be *true art*. 'Otherwise it will be impossible for it to exercise on the minds of those who listen to it (or sing it) that efficacy which the Church aims at obtaining in admitting into her liturgy the art of musical sound'. One wonders *what* some music of recent times exercises on the minds and hearts of those who sing it or hear it. What it comes to is that liturgical music must be authentic having 'goodness of form' and an 'aptitude for signifying that reality which is itself good and perfect. For the benefit which the Church seeks to derive from music is not that of aesthetic pleasure which music may give, but the *spiritual elevation* of the mind which it can cause'. Ultimately, music married to the word, is intended to lead people into the sacred mystery, the mystery of Christ who suffered, died and rose again to lead us into union with God. Thus, liturgical music excludes 'all works by which man attempts *only* to bring back to himself his own familiar universe'.[9] This is not to say that the liturgy should abstract itself from the concerns of the human race or that the poor of the Third World should attempt to 'forget' their needs and their wretchedness. These they express in their worship, appealing to Jesus Christ, Saviour and liberator, to rescue them from their plight. It is for them to find expressions that are appropriate to their situation.

Music of course concerns composers and if they are to compose for the liturgy they need first to understand the nature of the texts they are setting. There are lyrical texts like the Sanctus and the Gloria which latter is a series of acclamations. There are suppliant texts like the Kyrie and the Agnus Dei, both of which were parts of a litany and need to be treated as such. There are entrance texts (which need not always be hymns) and the communion psalm and both these are supposed to be sung by the people. The right sort of compositions can both enable and assist the assembly to sing them. And of course there is the responsorial psalm which links the first reading with the gospel and by its nature demands to be sung. This may be done in various ways but the people should always be allowed to sing the responses. If all these texts are treated in the right way, the people will then be singing and celebrating the Mass. The Constitution shows the way: 'They (musicians) should see that their compositions should not be of a kind that can be sung only by large choirs; they should also be suitable for smaller choirs and *encourage active participation on the part of the whole congregation*' (No 121).

It is sometimes said that music enhances the word but that needs understanding. It may seem to mean that music is a mere decoration of the words and that is sometimes how it has been used. 'Enhance' should be thought of as strengthening and enriching the message of the words. Some words indeed demand music. There is nothing duller than a *said* Alleluia. It is a cry of praise to the Lord: Hallel-Yah (shortened form of Yahweh): 'Praise God'. *Said* psalms – they are meant to be sung – lack a whole dimension. The Sanctus is, as I have said, an exultant acclamation of God in which the earthly church joins with the heavenly court in

responding with thanksgiving to the mighty works of God's salvation. *Said* it conveys very little and one could wish that it was
sung at every Mass. If four or five settings which could be sung
by the people, with perhaps support from a choir or cantor, were
devised and of such sort as could be easily learnt, they could be
used throughout the year at every Mass. The same could be
done for the Alleluias. As for the Gloria there are already several
acceptable settings which are in use and they are for the most
part acclamatory in style. Lastly, the Amen at the end of the eucharistic prayer demands song and if it is a threefold Amen it
can be made musically very effective, evoking in fact the response of the people who thus confirm and give their assent to
all that has been said and done during that prayer. In these ways
there can be real participation in the Mass by the people which is
all more effective if led and supported by a choir that knows
what it is for.

As we have seen in various pages the Church through the centuries has sought to control music in the liturgy by rejecting
what was unworthy and encouraging what is appropriate.
Though I am not in favour of control of the authoritarian style
and aware that legislation about the music to be sung in church
is a matter of great delicacy, there would seem to be a case for an
examination of what is going on in our churches with a view to
weeding out what is poor, bad or indifferent. To repeat, it is not
just a matter of taste – though there has been a sharp decline in
aesthetic appreciation – but of setting criteria for what is appropriate and what is not. In the long run it is a matter of education
and in England in the Catholic church there is too little musical
education. Above all, the liturgical and pastoral needs of the
people must be kept in mind. If they are to worship God with
mind and heart and body and voice, they must be allowed to
sing, helped to sing and encouraged to sing the praises of the
Lord.

If it be asked whether there were any shining musical lights, we
have to go first into the past. For an Augustine the chants for the
psalms in which the people could join were deeply moving. The
hymns composed by St Ambrose were sung by the people as
was the hymn, called a Sequence, the *Veni Sancte Spiritus* written
by Stephen Langton in the thirteenth century. The chant for the
Lamentations (attributed to Jeremiah) and once sung in ancient

style at the night office of the last three days of Holy Week (but, alas, no longer are) were high points of liturgical music to which the people responded with the *Convertere Jerusalem* (Turn to the Lord, Jerusalem). Coming to more recent times, the work of the Solesmes monks in restoring the plainchant led to a long-lost appreciation of a form of music that in a deep sense was an enhancement of the verbal texts. Finally, the promotion of congregational singing through the plainchant by Pius X and Pius XI brought back to vast numbers of people an understanding of active participation by the people through the singing of the chants of the Mass. Whether or not the plainchant can still be sung is a question but it can hardly be denied that its restoration brought about a new appreciation of what can be fittingly be sung in liturgical celebrations.

Notes

1. Confessions, X, (50), trans Henry Chadwick (OUP, 1992), p 208.

2. See Gregory Murray, OSB, *Choral Chants of the Mass*, published by the Society of St Gregory, 1947, p 3).

3. See Murray, op cit, pp 1, 10, 11, 14, 24, 25, 28, 29, 30, 31.

4. See Joseph Gelineau, *Voices and Instruments in Christian Worship*. Translated by Clifford Howell, SJ, The Liturgical Press, Collegeville, MN, 1964, p 195.

5. Gelineau, op cit, p 145.

6. Gelineau, op cit, p 49.

7. Gelineau, op cit, p 49, quoting from the XXII Session of the council.

8. See Gelineau, op cit, pp 52-3.

9. Gelineau, op cit, p 53 and notes 73b, 74. The insertion 'only' is mine.

CHAPTER XVI

A Brief Sketch of the Liturgical Movement (1909-1962)

The difficulties posed by a Latin and very rigidly ordered liturgy have been described in previous chapters. The efforts of those who pressed for some improvement may seem to have come to nothing. However in the nineteenth century a change came that had far reaching consequences, undreamed of by its originator.

It is generally agreed that the liturgical movement began with the work of Abbot Guéranger in France after he had restored the ancient abbey of Solesmes in the 1830s. His motives have been briefly sketched out in the previous chapter and some account of his at times questionable activities has been given. One thing cannot be doubted, he had a great love of the Roman liturgy as it then was. To him the 'Neo-Gallican' and, as he thought, the Jansenising liturgy of the eighteenth century was anathema; it must be destroyed and replaced by the Roman liturgy celebrated exactly and according to the approved Roman books. It must be said that he largely achieved this, though in the process he alienated bishops and destroyed much that was ancient and good.

All this however is not what he is remembered for. His two great works were the establishment of the monastery of Solesmes which was to become a nursery of liturgical scholars and the publication of his many-volumed *Anneé Liturgique*. In this he took the whole of the Liturgical Year for his field, commenting on the liturgical texts, illustrating them with others from different (including Eastern) liturgies and leading readers to prayer by the texts that he inserted. It was translated into many European languages and initiated vast numbers of people into an understanding of the liturgy as celebrated throughout the year.

The monastic and liturgical renewal at Solesmes attracted attention and had its influence first in other monasteries in France and then further afield. The two Wolter brothers, first secular priests in Germany and then professed monks at St Pauls-out-side-the-Walls in Rome, came to Solesmes and one after another learned the Benedictine way of life as it was practised there. They went back to Germany and founded the monastery of Beuron. From Dom Anselm Schott of that community in 1884 came the famous Messbuch (the missal in German) for the laity, that ran through many editions and is still in circulation, re-edited according to the Roman Missal of 1970. A group of Beuron monks founded Maredsous in Belgium in 1872, and from there the abbey of Mont-César at Louvain was founded. It was Dom Gérard van Caloen of Maredsous who produced his *Missel des Fidèles* in 1882 though the Ordinary of the Mass and the Canon were not translated. Van Caloen was a great admirer of Guéranger. The ground seemed to be prepared for another step forward and that would be taken before so very long.

In 1903 Pius X issued his *Motu proprio* on church music which contained the germinal phrase that the active participation of the people in the liturgy, the Mass and the Divine Office, was the indispensable source of the true Christian Spirit. Participation by the people through the singing of a restored plainsong became the programme for several decades to come though it must be admitted that progress was patchy and never achieved complete success. The phrase however resonated in the mind of a young priest who was deeply involved in working for miners in Liège. After eight years as a secular priest he entered the abbey of Mont-César and after profession was asked to lecture in theology. Whether officially or unofficially, he included a good deal of material on the liturgy. However, it was at a congress at Malines in 1909 that with some difficulty he managed to get a paper on the liturgy included in the programme. Dom Lambert Beauduin, for such was his name, received eloquent backing from the learned historian, a layman, Godefroid Kurth which was enthusiastically endorsed by Cardinal Mercier and other important authorities. Assisted by his brethren at Mont-César Beauduin got to work immediately. A popular publication *Le Vie Liturgique* appeared two months after the congress and this by 1911 had become *Questions liturgiques* which after more than eighty years is still very much alive. The first *Semaine liturgique* had already been held in 1910 and continued until the war of 1914 when Belgium was ravaged by the German army. It was in that same year that Beauduin had provided the theological basis for the new pastoral liturgical movement. In his *La Piété de l'Eglise* he established that the priesthood of Christ (in which all the baptised participate) and the Church as the mystical body of Christ (i.e., emphasis on community) were the foundations of a renewed liturgical practice.

The war brought all this to an end but it was taken up again in 1918. Belgium remained the principal centre of the liturgical movement. The *Semaines liturgiques* continued year after year and their published proceedings produced a body of doctrine and information which was without equal in its time. It was in Belgium that the movement known as the Young Christian Workers was founded by Father (later Cardinal) Cardijn and it was they who brought the liturgical movement to the sort of people Dom Lambert had first served and it was they who gave the practice of the Dialogue Mass a great impetus. This was a way of making active participation accessible to everyone and on all sorts of occasions. The assembly responded and said the Gloria, Sanctus etc., with the priest. This practice was put to Rome in 1922 and the request for permission was treated by the Congregation of Rites in frosty style. The officials obviously did not like it and refrained only from total prohibition. In reply to another request on the same matter from the Archbishop of Genoa in 1935, the tone was more friendly and the practice was permitted. The responsibility for organising the Dialogue Mass was, quite properly, laid upon diocesan bishops. Meanwhile all this and offertory processions had been going on in Belgium and, as the Young Christian Workers movement spread to France, also in that country.

With the arrival of Abbot Ildefonse Herwegen as Abbot of Maria-Laach in 1913 his monastery (of the Beuron congregation) began to be a centre of the liturgical movement. As in Belgium and France the war intervened but when it was over, Maria-Laach not only continued its work but expanded it. Members of the educated classes, what one might call the intelligentsia, were invited to the monastery where they learned the meaning of the liturgy and took part in the celebration of the liturgy in the ancient Carolingian church (with the altar facing the assembly) as well as being familiarised with the Dialogue Mass. Concurrently the abbot and his community initiated two learned periodicals and a more popular series called *Ecclesia Orans* of which the first volume was the well known *The Spirit of the Liturgy* (ET, 1930) by Romano Guardini, who in spite of his name was a German.

In Austria Pius Parsch, an Augustinian Canon, who like Beauduin, had learnt of the spiritual poverty of ordinary Catholic men through his experiences as an army chaplain, began a similar work at Klosterneuburg, near Vienna. He developed the *Betsingmesse* and, through his paper *Bibel und Liturgie*, strongly emphasised the need for biblical knowledge. By his several-volumed book, *The Year of Salvation*, translated into several languages, and his studies on the Mass and the Divine Office, he propagated sound information on the liturgy which became widely known through-out the world.

He was in touch with the monastery of Maria-Laach in Germany where, as said above, Abbot Herwegen with Dom Odo Casel was making it a centre of liturgical thinking and theology. In the 1920s the latter began working out his theology of the 'mystery-presence' of Christ and his salvation in the celebration of the liturgy. This too was a germinal moment for though Casel's views were contested for many years his emphasis on the Paschal Mystery (the passion, death and resurrection of Christ) as the dynamic heart of the liturgy can be discerned as forming the basis of the Constitution on the Liturgy. When the Nazis took power in 1933 and the church in Germany was gradually restricted in its activities, the bishops and priests found in a re-newed understanding and practice of the liturgy a source of great strength for the people.

Directly inspired by Pius X's *Motu proprio* and the *Divini Cultus* of Pius X in 1928 there came the English Society of St Gregory founded by Dom Bernard McElligott of Ampleforth Abbey in 1929. Its aim was to promote the active participation of the peo-ple in the liturgy largely through the singing in plainsong of those parts of the Mass that belong to them. It continued its work even during the Second World War (except for one year's intermission when Britain was being badly bombed) and one Mass during the week was always a Dialogue Mass. The use of the Dialogue Mass had indeed been spreading in boarding and other schools, many of the young people in the forces were familiar with it and when the army chaplains, themselves young, came to minister to the troops they propagated the Dialogue Mass. To sing Mass was out of the question but here were these young men facing danger and death, and for them the Eucharist was of paramount importance. So the chaplains took it up, whether the bishops liked it or not. There was in England as elsewhere a great stirring during the war, much was being questioned, old 'traditions', which were not so very old, were being examined and when the war was over the young people, now no longer so young, wanted to continue to do what they had been doing in the forces. They were not always satisfied with what they found back home![1]

The Second World War brought death and untold suffering to countless thousands of people yet out of it came the beginnings of an extraordinary renewal of the Church. It seems to have acted as a catalyst for the liturgical movement. France was occupied by the German army and it seemed that France would be incorporated into Germany. There was free passage between the two countries and the French and the German liturgists came together exchanged ideas and began to form a strong if unofficial union. It was out of these meetings that emerged the Pastoral Liturgical Movement. Not only must the liturgy be made accessible to the people but it must be understood that the liturgy is not a clerical possession; it belongs to the whole Christian community. In the community of worship this must be demonstrated by the participation of the various ministers that go to make up the community: choir, servers, readers etc…. It is true that this did not fully come about until after Vatican II but the way was being prepared long before it.

Out of this situation was born in Paris the Centre de Pastorale Liturgique (1943) which stimulated and promoted a considerable number of activities, among them the annual congress, mostly of priests, at Versailles, and gatherings of French and Germans at St Odile in Alsace and at Maria-Laach in Germany which can be seen as the forerunners of the international congresses that met in later years, Lugano (1953) and, the most important of all, the Congress at Assisi (1956) which directly involved the Roman authorities. Another feature of this stage of the liturgical movement was the close collaboration of liturgists with scripture experts, systematic theologians, historians, and even sociologists. This in turn reflected a new situation in the Church. There was not only a liturgical revival, there was the

biblical revival and the ever-increasing activity of the ecu-
menists. Representatives of these currents of opinion all worked
together. It was a foreshadowing of the Second Vatican Council.

Long before this the liturgical movement had penetrated into
most parts of the Church. Dom Virgil Michel of St John's Abbey,
Collegeville, USA, had founded the review *Orate Fratres* (now
Worship) and gradually formed the conference of Benedictines
for the promotion of the liturgy. In 1940 the first of the great and
numerously attended 'Liturgical Weeks' took place in Chicago
and continued year after year until after 1961. Dom Michel's work
was continued very vigorously by Dom Godfrey Diekmann who
not only edited *Orate Fratres* but was very active promoting the
'Liturgical Weeks'. After the war he was able to travel in Europe
(which he already knew as he had studied in Rome and at Maria-
Laach before taking his doctorate in theology at Sant'Anselmo).
He got to know all the leaders of the liturgical movement in
Europe, he attended the great congresses of the 1950s and
poured vast amounts of information about the movement into
the pages of *Orate Fratres* which he re-named *Worship*. Greatly to
his delight, he was appointed a *peritus* to the Preparatory Commission to the Second Vatican Council and with his friend Mgr
Fred McManus made a considerable impact. He was well prepared by his own scholarship and by his knowledge of what was
going on in Europe and elsewhere.[2]

As recorded in a previous chapter, the Italian movement was
gradually making its way. In England just after the Second
World War, after a long and sometimes heated public controversy in the Catholic press, Fr S. J. Gosling founded the society for
the Use of English in the Liturgy and a few years later a
Vernacular Society was founded in the USA. Ireland had its first
liturgical meeting at Glenstal Abbey in 1953, promoted by the
Benedictines and the Dominicans, and this became an annual
congress attracting large numbers and including international
lecturers. It also published its proceedings in a series of useful
volumes.

Most of the Catholic world had been touched by the liturgical
movement before Vatican II though its effectiveness was patchy.
As was shown after the 'changes in the liturgy' in the 1960s great
numbers were in no way prepared for them because their bish-

ops and priests had chosen to ignore the liturgical movement as well as the biblical and ecumenical movements. It was not as if there had been a sudden revolution or that, as some said, the Church had gone mad. It was that there had been a gradual development that can be said to have had its origin in the germinal phrase of Pius X's *Motu proprio* about the active participation of the people in liturgy. Quite rightly this is seen as the beginning of a pastoral liturgical movement which was put into effect by Dom Lambert Beauduin and his many co-operators and followers. For years the movement was faithful to the post-Tridentine liturgical books. There was no talk of reform or change but attitudes to and understanding of the liturgy did change or rather develop and that was all in accord with what those responsible for the liturgical movement wanted to effect. The people must be helped *to take part in the liturgy as it was* though it was not easy. Scholarship as well as pastoral practice in a changing world began to reveal that the rites as they existed were inadequate and made real participation difficult. This was felt not only in the celebration of the Mass but also in the celebration of the sacraments of baptism (infant), confirmation, marriage when the people are so intimately involved, and also in the funeral rites which all had to be in Latin.

Things had also been stirring in Rome, earlier than is generally known. In 1925 Pius XI, who had been trained in the rigorous disciplines of scholarship in the Ambrosiana at Milan, founded an Institute of Christian Archaeology where students gained a knowledge and love of the liturgy. He followed this up by creating the Historical Section of the Congregation of Rites which would have an important role to play later on. In 1947, after the Second World War, no doubt in response to the ever increasing activity of the liturgical movement, came Pius XII's encyclical *Mediator Dei*, on Christian Worship, which brought to the forefront once again the priesthood of the laity which they share with Christ the Priest and by its analysis of the rite of the Mass showed how it is, by its very structure, the action of a community. Though in some parts it was cautious, it undoubtedly supported the main thrust of the liturgical movement, especially in the matter of participation and gave much encouragement to those who had been promoting the liturgical movement for so long. It also contained another germinal phrase: 'The adoption of the vernacular in quite a number of functions may prove of great benefit to the faithful' (No 64). Co-incidentally or not, the same year appeared Rituals for France and Austria with some vernacular in the administration of the sacraments and other rites. Germany followed in 1948 and other countries gradually, England being among the last and with the smallest amount of the vernacular.

The pastoral clergy found this change a great boon but it also revealed the need for *reform*. Four exorcisms in the baptismal rite of infants were not only too many but raised questions about the propriety of exorcising infants at all. The rite of confirmation was jejune and said little to the young, and the meagre rite of marriage needed enriching. The total bann on any vernacular in the celebration of Mass was causing restiveness not only among those promoting the liturgical movement but among pastors of parishes and the young. Was it not right that the scriptures of the Mass should be able to make their immediate impact by being read in the language of the people? The Biblical Revival had been making its impact also. These and other questions were being discussed all over the Church and there was a widespread desire for reform. The only question that seemed open was what form it would take.

After his encyclical Pius XII set up a special commission to study and prepare proposals for the reform of the liturgy such as its members saw to be necessary. It was this commission, which included members of the Historical Section, that drew up the revised rite of the Easter Vigil first permitted in 1951 and, with consultation of leading liturgists, the revised liturgy of the whole of Holy Week (1955). Greeted with dismay by a few with enthusiasm by most, this work was a clear sign that liturgical reform was on its way.[3]

There were other signs coming from Rome. Evening Masses were permitted in 1953 and the fast before communion was shortened to three hours before receiving and later still to one hour. In 1955 the Decree on the *Simplification of the Rubrics* of the missal and the breviary was issued and in 1958 there appeared *The Instruction on Sacred Music and Sacred Liturgy* which suggested various ways of participation and permitted lay *men* to read the scripture readings at Mass in the vernacular (while the priest was saying them in Latin). It was a great step forward and long desired by the promoters of the liturgical movement. Finally, in 1960 came the *Corpus Rubricarum* of which Pope John XXIII said that it was a preface to the Vatican Council, which he had already summoned, and which would explore the principles that would lead to a reform (*instaurationem*) of the liturgy. As is well known, the Second Vatican Council met in the autumn of 1962. Hopes were high but fears were many. In the event because the ground had been so well prepared, the fears were dispelled and the hopes fulfilled. At the end of the international Congress on the Liturgy held at Assisi in 1956 Pius XII had said that the liturgical movement was a sign of the passage of the Holy Spirit on the Church (*sulla Chiesa*). This was amply fulfilled by the Council itself when it promulgated the Constitution on the Liturgy in 1963. One feels justified in saying that those who have resisted are insensitive to the working of the Holy Spirit in the Church.

Bibliography

The full history of the liturgical movement remains to be written. For the preparation of Vatican II see Annibale Bugnini, *The Reform of the Liturgy 1948–1975* (The Liturgical Press, Collegeville, MN, Ed. Matthew J. O'Connell, 1990). Many commentaries on the Constitution appeared in various languages, including the present writer's *The Church's Worship* (1964).

Notes

1. For the Liturgical Movement in England see *English Catholic Worship*, J.D. Crichton, H.E. Winstone, R. Ainslie, (eds). Geoffrey Chapman, London, 1979.

2. See *The Monk's Tale. A Biography of Godfrey Diekmann, OSB* by Kathleen Hughes, RSCJ (The Liturgical Press, Collegeville, Minnesota, 1991). The book gives a good account of the liturgical movement in the USA though no doubt a fuller account will one day be written.

3. Some of the above information is not widely known. See *Notitiae* (the organ of the Congregation for Worship), no 324, July 1993, 7.

Index

Sergius I, Pope   100, 141
Shakespeare   137
Shape of the Liturgy   98
Siri, Giuseppe 127
Sirmium (Mitrovitza)   135
Society of the Sacred Mission, Kelham 88
Society of St Gregory   81
Söderblom, Bishop   90
Solesmes Abbey   151
Somerset, Duke of   104
Sorbonne   52, 66
Southwark   84
South Kensington Museum   84
Spain   25, 42, 131, 132
Spirit of the Liturgy   The 154
Stations of the Cross, The   122
Sursum corda   89
Sweden, Church of   89
Stafford, Vicount   67
St Barnabas, Church of   78
St Chad, Church of   78
St Charles College, Bayswater 111
St Edmund's College   83, 115
Stevenson, Kenneth   101
St Giles, Church of   77
St Hugh, Church of   114
St John's Abbey, Collegeville, USA 156
St Odile, Alsace   155
Storia Liturgica   128
St Pauls-outside-the-Walls, Rome 152
Stuttgart, Chapel of   41
Subiaco 128
Summa Theologiae   25
Switzerland 124
Synod   33, 34
Synod of Pistoia   30ff, 33, 34, 48

Taizé 147
Talbot, John   83
Tamburini, Fortunato   17, 18, 20
Te Deum   132
Tertullian   95, 121, 131, 132